VISIBLE
OPS
SECURITY

ACHIEVING COMMON SECURITY AND IT OPERATIONS OBJECTIVES IN 4 PRACTICAL STEPS

IT Process Institute

Authors

GENE KIM
PAUL LOVE
GEORGE SPAFFORD

First Edition published March 2008. Third printing May 2010. Printed in the United States of America.

"Visible Ops Security" is part of the Visible Ops series published by the IT Process Institute, Inc.

For more information contact:

IT Process Institute, Inc
2896 Crescent Avenue
Suite 104
Eugene, OR 97408
Main Telephone: (541) 485-4051
Main Fax: (541) 485-8163
http://www.itpi.org
info@itpi.org
ISBN: 978-0-9755686-2-0

Credits

Managing Editor: Kurt Milne
Project Coordinator: Mary Matthews
Copy Editors: Mangione, Payne & Associates
Book Design: Integrity Design and Marketing, Portland, Oregon

Acknowledgements

The IT Process Institute offers a special thank you to a number of important contributors. Without the knowledge, hard work, and dedication of the following individuals, we would be challenged to produce the important tools which help to shape IT for our time.

Scott Alldridge	Steve Darby	Ron Neumann
Julia Allen	Jeff Foucher	Stephen Northcutt
Jennifer Bayuk	Ron Gula	Peter Perfetti
Richard Bejtlich	Glenn Hyatt	Sasha Romanosky
Brian Bell	Donna Knapp	Mark Sanman
James Bohem	Norman Marks	A.J. Schwab
Sumner Blount	Dwayne Melancon	Jay Taylor
Gavin Bromfield	Craig Morgan	Jeff Weber

About The IT Process Institute:

The IT Process Institute (ITPI) is an independent research organization that exists to support the membership of IT operations, security, and audit professionals. Our mission is to advance IT management science through independent research, benchmarking, and the development of prescriptive guidance. Our primary objective is to identify common practices that are proven to improve the performance of IT organizations. With a simple data-driven and participatory approach, the IT Process Institute aims to uncover unique insights that boost the efficiency and effectiveness of our member organizations.

ITPI is a membership based organization. We are a group of concerned and involved IT practitioners that are committed to improving the operating performance of IT organizations across all industries. Funded by the generous sponsorship of leading organizations, and reasonable membership fees, ITPI is able to fund both projects and ongoing operations.

The IT Process Institute has created a unique three-part methodology designed to leverage a shared-cost model that enables top-performing capabilities through the participation of our members.

- **Research**—participate in the identification and study top-performers through qualitative and quantitative methods.
- **Benchmarking**—leverage tools that allow members to compare their practices and results to the top performing organizations identified in our studies.
- **Prescriptive Guidance**—share individual practices that offer applied insights from research findings and benchmark results.

The IT Process Institute provides an alternative source of information for IT decision makers. Our shared research model allows participating organizations to receive data about what is proven to work, and that is shared among those participating in the research. And, through participation, provide opportunities for IT practitioners to help direct and shape the research to meet specific requirements of their organizations.

- **Focused**—we are not tied to existing industry frameworks. Our obsession is simply discovering what works.
- **Data driven**—we believe in a data driven approach to performance improvement, and use empirical research as the cornerstone for our products and services.
- **Designed to enable top levels of performance**—The IT Process Institute enables competitive advantage by focusing on the causes of top performance, which we define as the top 15th percentile of organizations we study.

The study data used to support the research behind the Visible Ops Security methodology is available to IT and security practitioners as benchmarking tools. These self assessment tools cover a range of operational topics and can be purchased for use on the ITPI website.

Learn more about the IT Process Institute by visiting www.itpi.org

Testimonials:

"Visible Ops Security is the first work I've found that helps connect all the dots between the shared objectives held by management, security professionals, auditors, and IT professionals. This is so important since all of us, regardless of profession, are often guilty of pursuing the 'green' on our own scorecards without linking those metrics to shared goals and what is most important to the organization overall.

It is clear that top performing IT organizations have found ways to simultaneously advance the goals of all the key groups: information security, IT operations, development, and audit. Many organizations, both large and small, will find the practical and clear guidance in Visible Ops Security to be very compelling in helping their efforts to get ahead of the risk management, compliance, and governance curve.

This book is very readable, much like a novel. It is written in such a way that the reader will feel like they are discussing the issues with others in their IT shop. Visible Ops Security takes the reader on a safari of sorts, first telling him where to pitch his tent to secure the 'base camp' for future operations, then giving him a map to take his canoe on the hunt up the river to the land of Development and Deployment, all the while avoiding the nasty alligators and piranha along the way."
—JAY R. TAYLOR, CIA, CISA, CFE, GENERAL DIRECTOR, GLOBAL IT AUDIT & FINANCIAL SERVICES AUDIT, GENERAL MOTORS CORPORATION

"This book has many groundbreaking insights, but my favorites are the 'Tone from the Top' and 'Define the Consequences' sections. Everyone involved in the creation, review, or approval of policy should be able to quote these sections verse by verse."
—STEPHEN NORTHCUTT, SANS INSTITUTE

"The Visible Ops Security handbook should be on the must-read list of all managers and CxOs who are involved with IT, data leakage, and compliance. It provides a play-by-play walk-through for how IT and security can work together towards the common goals of the business without getting in each other's way and without creating bureaucracy."—RON GULA, CTO AND COFOUNDER, TENABLE NETWORK SECURITY

"When I heard a Visible Ops Security book was in the works, I was skeptical about the need for a sequel to the original Visible Ops. But Visible Ops Security isn't a sequel. It's an essential companion to the original Visible Ops book."
—STEVE DARBY, VP OF OPERATIONS, IP SERVICES

"Visible Ops Security provides the clearest recommendations for improving and sustaining an organization's security operations that I have yet seen. It advocates integrating with, not circumventing, existing IT and business processes. It doesn't advocate security for security's sake but properly recognizes the business purpose for appropriate security policies. The authors are clearly skilled in information security and IT methodologies, and Visible Ops Security reflects this knowledge and experience."
—SASHA ROMANOSKY, CARNEGIE MELLON UNIVERSITY

"All auditors interested in information security should read and think about the messages in this very readable, well-written book. Not only will they understand what works in information security, but also they can use it to optimize the design of their audit work. Effective control each day keeps the auditors away!"
—NORMAN D. MARKS, VICE PRESIDENT INTERNAL AUDIT, BUSINESS OBJECTS S.A.

"This is an excellent guide to building a successful IT infrastructure from a security perspective. The authors have masterfully articulated the methodologies used successfully by many of us in security and risk management and I can personally validate their findings. The four phases outlined here provide the framework to stabilize, secure, manage, and improve the security of your IT infrastructure."
—PETER PERFETTI, DIRECTOR, IT SECURITY AND RISK MANAGEMENT

"At last, a book clearly and concisely illustrating that security, operations, and development are complementary, not mutually exclusive. Valuable information presented at a high enough level to enable executives to make sound strategic decisions, but with enough practical detail for tactical managers to execute with confidence. A must have reference for all those seeking to attain a high degree of 'secure by design, not afterthought' in operational and development processes."
—GAVIN BROMFIELD, SENIOR ITSM CONSULTANT, PEPPERWEED CONSULTING LLC

"The book examines what IT security organizations do well and their common struggles. A must read for those in security and audit who seek improvement, but also important and informative for those who work closely with security in business processes, accounting, auditing, development, and operations. The authors understand the problems that keep many IT security organizations from reaching effectiveness or potential, and disarm perceptions that hold these organizations back by offering clear steps to move out of the trenches to the top of their games."
—JAMES BOHEM, CISSP, ENTERPRISE SECURITY SOLUTIONS ARCHITECT, MIS SYSTEMS INTEGRATORS

"As an auditor and an IT practitioner, I have repeatedly seen solution-oriented behaviors transform technologists into business partners. Visible Ops Security provides a realistic approach to converting information security from a technical function into a business function."—A.J. SCHWAB, SENIOR IT AUDIT MANAGER

"In my work with IT organizations around the world, the difference between effective and ineffective IT security organizations is profound. This book captures the essence of those differences and provides actionable steps that any organization can implement to become great, and dramatically increase security's value to the business."
—DWAYNE MELANCON, CISA

"Devising and deploying an effective security infrastructure is a major challenge, especially as the requirements for regulatory compliance continue to multiply for large enterprises. There are both significant technical and organizational challenges that need to be met in order to ensure that the security policies are effective, and meeting the needs of the business. Security Visible Ops is an excellent resource for both the Security and Operations teams, as it provides real-life and proven techniques for improving the overall effectiveness of any security initiative."
—SUMNER BLOUNT, DIRECTOR OF SECURITY SOLUTIONS, CA

"Organizations striving to optimize information security face many similar challenges. The first is ensuring security is considered long before IT services are implemented in production. The second is ensuring the information security process offers the right amount of control, without introducing excessive bureaucracy. Visible Ops Security is an engaging, highly readable book that meets these challenges head on. It offers a pragmatic approach that ensures development, information security and IT operations staff work together throughout the service lifecycle. It also offers a step-by-step roadmap that, while specific in nature, encourages a bigger picture perspective aimed at ensuring business objectives are met."
—DONNA KNAPP, CURRICULUM DEVELOPMENT MANAGER, ITSM ACADEMY

Foreword:

Today, all we have to do is read the headlines to find attention-grabbing examples of how inadequate information, applications, and IT security can impact our businesses. There is documented evidence that security breaches can affect brand, marketplace trust, customer privacy and identity, and the bottom line. The proliferation of security laws and regulations demand an increasing share of our attention and effort, with escalating consequences for noncompliance.

Answering the question "How much security is enough?" is a tough proposition. Security is hard to put your finger on. It does not reside in a particular location and is accomplished through a diverse combination of people, process, and technology controls. Adequate security for any given product, service, or organization is determined based on tolerance for risk—easy to say, hard to quantify, and constantly changing.

While we're trying to get our heads around these complex issues and make sure we're not the next press release (or court case!), there are a set of proven, sound practices that allow enterprise IT operations and security teams to effectively operate and maintain production systems and meet security-based compliance requirements while providing new business-driven services.

Visible Ops Security derives from years of operational experience, customer engagements, and rigorous research and benchmarking performed by the IT Process Institute. Working with top performing organizations to tease out what differentiates them from medium and low-performers, the authors have found that high-performing security teams have unique cultural characteristics (trust with IT, understand business context, and foster cooperation) and attributes (business aligned, plugged in, add value, understand priorities, and are people savvy).

Based on this research, *Visible Ops Security* identifies 4 phases for integrating information security into development and operations so that it becomes business as usual. The steps for each phase offer a prescriptive sequence of measurable actions, supported by true life examples that readers can easily identify with and use to help build momentum and support. By working together, development, security, and IT are in a better position to achieve common objectives and demonstrate business value.

As a community, we are way past due in making common sense common practice by deploying known solutions to known problems. If you are feeling the pain of siloed IT operations and security efforts, turf battles, suboptimal performance, and limited capacity to add new services, and if you have the energy, attention span, and collective will to implement one proven approach, *Visible Ops Security* is a great place to start!

Julia Allen
Senior Member of the Technical Staff
Carnegie Mellon University, Software Engineering Institute, CERT® Program

Table of Contents

Introduction

Senior executives in information security, information technology (IT), and in the business served by IT are often very concerned about securing and safeguarding IT systems and data—particularly those systems and data critical to the business. However, leadership is often challenged to rationalize the amount of time and resources to invest in information security, especially when the risks seem obscure or difficult to understand. This is, in large part, due to structural issues related to the creation, day-to-day management, and oversight of the information security function, where the potential security risks are seemingly infinite, but resources to counter the risks are definitely finite.

Today, because of high-profile information security failures, there is an ever increasing number of external forces mandating security in the IT environment. The Sarbanes-Oxley (SOX) Act of 2002, the Gramm-Leach-Bliley Act, Health Insurance Portability and Accountability Act (HIPAA), emerging privacy laws, and the Payment Card Industry Data Security Standard (PCI DSS) are just a few examples of external regulatory and contractual requirements with a compulsory information security component. Failure to have adequate information security controls in place can put the organization at risk of losing confidentiality, integrity, and availability of data and IT services. This can then put the organization at risk for financial penalties, brand damage, lawsuits, etc.

To safeguard the organization, the business and IT must integrate sustainable information security practices into IT operational and service development[1] processes. Responsibility for making this happen falls directly on the shoulders of the information security team, as mandated by senior management. However, information security is typically not directly responsible for the IT operational or service development functions. Consequently, for information security practitioners to meet their objectives, they must also influence other groups by adding value and helping them achieve their objectives and the business[2] goals. In order to remain sustainable and viable in the organization, information security must transition from being merely a management edict to being an integral part of daily business operations.

This handbook builds upon *The Visible Ops Handbook: Implementing ITIL in 4 Practical And Auditable Steps (2004)* which has been widely embraced and adopted by IT operations. *Visible Ops Security* expands the methodology to show how to integrate information security and compliance objectives into day-to-day IT operations, IT service development, project management, release management, and internal audit.

---

[1] This book uses the term *IT service development* or *service development* instead of *software development* or *application development*, to reinforce that IT services require more than just software (e.g., hardware, documentation, legal contracts, etc.).

[2] The terms *business* and *business goals* include private-sector enterprises as well as nonprofit organizations and government entities.

Visible Ops Security describes how information security professionals can break through organizational silos and enable information security by:

- Ensuring that information security focuses on protecting what matters to the organization, and then embedding information security controls into daily operations of change management, access management and incident management. This will enable us to deter unauthorized changes, reduce the likelihood of unauthorized access, reduce efforts around audit preparation, remediation, and shorten the time required to detect and correct information security incidents.

- Ensuring that information security controls add value to the business and other IT stakeholders, by helping them achieve their functional goals and objectives. By doing this, information security builds and reinforces a culture of controls, helping the organization better manage risk. This includes:
  — Safeguarding confidential customer information
  — Protecting against fraud
  — Protecting brand and reputation
  — Maximizing revenue through highly available business systems
  — Safeguarding revenue by protecting against errors and malicious acts
  — Ensuring timely and accurate financial reporting

- Proactively integrating information security into upstream activities, such as project management, development and release management processes. This enables us to build quality into releases, reducing the likelihood of future information security incidents.

The Visible Ops Handbook and *Visible Ops Security* are based on the study of the common practices of high-performing IT organizations. Since *The Visible Ops Handbook* was published, the IT Process Institute has studied and benchmarked more than 850 IT organizations to gain deeper insights into what enables high performers to excel. This research validates many of the information security-related practices outlined in the original handbook, and shows that high-performing information security and IT operations groups often achieve their performance breakthroughs using the same approaches and techniques.

The Visible Ops Handbook has been widely cited as one of the best resources for building sustainable and auditable controls by IT operations practitioners. However, the authors often received feedback that the security benefits of IT controls should be emphasized more. As a result, the authors were motivated to do further research and write *Visible Ops Security*.

Among the goals of *Visible Ops Security* is to describe how to build repeatable and verifiable IT processes that are necessary for information security to succeed. The book prescriptively describes the steps for transforming information security from "good to great" by integrating with other functional groups.

Something Needs Improvement—Otherwise Why Read This?

The motivations for securing the IT environment are well known. However, truly integrating information security into other functional groups is complicated by a variety of challenges.

When things go wrong in IT, there is a tendency for information security, IT operations, and development to blame each other. Information security may blame IT operations or development, who may blame information security in return. Each group believes the other is obstructing its efforts because their interactions are often limited to situations in which one group is demanding something of the other. To make matters worse, each group often perceives that there is a long history of the other groups obstructing or undoing its work.

Described below are two typical categories of challenges, each of which is addressed in the *Visible Ops Security* methodology. The first category of problems describes how typical service development and IT operational practices complicate life for information security. For example:

- IT service and infrastructure components may be deployed to production in an inherently insecure and unsupportable state. Information security must then address deficiencies after the fact, when the cost of remediating the deficiencies is higher than if they had been discovered and addressed earlier in the life cycle. If not addressed, both information security and IT operations, and ultimately the organization, suffer the consequences over time in higher operating costs, information security incidents, audit findings, brand damage, and so forth.

- Development projects may be constantly behind schedule, in part because information security requirements are added late in the project life cycle. To preserve project due date and budget commitments, the information security requirements may be ignored or marginalized. And this is even assuming that information security is even aware that the project exists!

- The state of the production IT infrastructure is often complex and not well understood. The lack of a preproduction test environment that adequately mirrors production makes predicting outcomes of both information security and operational changes difficult, if not impossible. As a result, IT personnel may operate in a patch-and-pray mode, where no one knows with any certainty what the outcomes of their changes will be in production.

- Portions of the IT infrastructure in the production environment are known to be fragile, so implementing any changes to these services is likely to cause an incident. To "secure" these components, information security typically resorts to Google, tribal knowledge, and best guesses to identify stop-gap measures. These fragile artifacts are rarely, if ever, replaced or patched due to fear of the unknown.

- Lack of information security standards increases project effort and cost, because previous security work cannot be reused and leveraged. This increases the effort required for information security, development, and IT operations to design, develop, review, test, approve, and maintain these IT services.

- Poor availability of IT services sets off audit red flags, increasing scrutiny and causing urgent unplanned work. When IT operations and information security staff are constantly in firefighting mode, neither have time to complete planned work — such as replacing fragile artifacts, fixing information security vulnerabilities or otherwise moving the organization towards its goal.

- IT operations people use shared accounts to simplify access and password issues, jeopardizing security objectives and auditability.

- IT operations people are busy with their own issues, and do not address known information security vulnerabilities at the rate that information security wants.

However, in the second category of problems, information security impedes the achievement of the goals of IT operations and development. For example:

- Information security controls often have a reputation for creating bureaucracy that hampers the completion of new projects. When doing things correctly takes too long or information security requirements are considered too late in the project life cycle, the business survival instinct forces everyone to go around the information security requirements to meet the budget and schedule needs.

- When information security has a sufficiently large backlog of reviews of changes and projects, information security becomes part of the critical path for projects to complete. Often, large, high-profile projects are ready to be deployed, but a last-minute firewall change request delays the project two weeks while it goes through the information security review and change management process. Suddenly, information security is viewed as an obstacle and a bottleneck that is slowing the business down.

- Implementation of information security requirements introduces delays in project timelines, reinforcing the perception by the business that information security lacks a sense of urgency and does not appreciate date and cost targets.

- Business and other functional groups complain that correcting issues identified during information security reviews costs too much, takes too long, and reduces the feature sets needed by the business. Information security is then viewed as a constant liability to the business, instead of a contributing asset.

- When security fixes are actually implemented (either project related or urgent patches), they often adversely impact production systems. For instance, a security patch is deployed that causes 20 percent of the systems to crash and 5 percent of the systems to no longer reboot. The political ramifications are significant.

The Study Of High-Performing IT Organizations

The Visible Ops Handbook was the culmination of a four-year study of the common practices of high-performing IT organizations that started in early 2000. These organizations were simultaneously achieving world-class results in IT operations as measured by high service availability, information security as measured by early and consistent integration into the IT service delivery life cycle, and compliance as measured by the fewest number of repeat audit findings.

Astoundingly, these organizations were also the most efficient as measured by server-to-system administrator ratio and the amount of time spent on unplanned work. The provocative conclusion is that integrating controls into daily operations results not only in effectiveness, but also efficiency!

The Visible Ops Handbook codified how to replicate the three cultures that were common among the high-performing IT organizations exhibited:

- A culture of change management—In each of the high-performing IT organizations, the first step when IT staff implements changes is not to first log into the infrastructure. Instead, it is to go to some change advisory board and get authorization that the change should be made. Surprisingly, this process is not viewed as bureaucratic, needlessly slowing things down, lowering productivity, and decreasing the quality of life. Instead, these organizations view change management as absolutely critical to the organization for maintaining its high performance.

- A culture of causality—Each of the high-performing IT organizations has a common way to resolve service outages and impairments. They realize that 80 percent of their outages are due to changes, and that 80 percent of their mean time to repair (MTTR) is spent trying to find what changed. Consequently, when working problems, they look at changes first in the repair cycle. Evidence of this can be seen in the incident management systems of the high performers: Inside the incident record for an outage are all the scheduled and authorized changes for the affected assets, as well as the actual detected changes on the asset. By looking at this information, problem managers can recommend a fix to the problem more than 80 percent of the time, with a first fix rate exceeding 90 percent (i.e., 90 percent of the recommended fixes work the first time).

- A culture of planned work and continuous improvement—In each of the high-performing IT organizations, there is a continual desire to find production variance early before it causes a production outage or an episode of unplanned work. The difference is analogous to paying attention to the low-fuel warning light on an automobile to avoid running out of gas on the highway. In the first case, the organization can fix the problem in a planned manner, without much urgency or disruption to other scheduled work. In the second case, the organization must fix the problem in a highly urgent way, often requiring an all-hands-on-deck situation (e.g., six staff members must drop everything they are doing and run down the highway with gas cans to refuel the stranded truck.)

The IT Process Institute has continued to identify and research the distinguishing characteristics of high-performing IT organizations. A series of research projects conducted in conjunction with organizations such as the Software Engineering Institute at Carnegie Mellon University, the Institute of Internal Auditors Research Foundation, and GCR Insights, have concentrated on identifying the practices and performance that distinguish high-performers across more than 850 IT organizations studied.

The 2006 and 2007 ITPI IT Controls Performance Study was conducted to establish the link between controls and operational performance. The 2007 Change Configuration and Release Performance Study was conducted to determine which best practices in these areas drive performance improvement. The studies revealed that, in comparison with low-performing organizations, high-performing organizations enjoy the following efficiency advantages:

- Production system changes fail half as often.
- Releases cause unintended failures half as often.
- One quarter of the frequency of emergency change requests.
- One quarter the frequency of repeat audit findings.
- One half the amount of unplanned work and firefighting.
- Server-to-system-administrator ratios are two times higher.

These differences validate that the Visible Ops hypothesis that IT controls and basic change and configuration practices improve IT operations effectiveness and efficiency. But, the studies also determined that the same high performers have superior information security effectiveness, as well. The 2007 IT controls study found that when high performers had security breaches:

- The security breaches are far less likely to result in loss events (e.g., financial, reputational, and customer). High performers are half as likely as medium performers and one-fifth as likely as low performers to experience security breaches that result in loss.
- The security breaches are far more likely to be detected using automated controls (as opposed to an external source such as the newspaper headlines or a customer). High performers automatically detect security breaches 15 percent more often than medium performers and twice as often as low performers.
- Security access breaches are detected far more quickly. High performers have a mean time to detect anomalies measured in minutes, compared with hours for medium performers and days for low performers.

These studies confirmed that high-performing IT organizations have figured out how to simultaneously advance the goals of information security and IT operations. They take proactive and decisive steps to promote teamwork. Information security works with IT operations to manage production systems efficiently and securely. Information security integrates with development to streamline the introduction of new systems into production, maintaining the security of these systems without introducing unnecessary controls or impeding development efforts significantly while still making sure that risks are properly managed.

In other words, the value of information security controls is not just loss avoidance and better information security incident handling. *Instead, implementing the right information security controls helps advance the goals not only of information security, but also of IT operations and development as well!*

In these high-performing organizations, all three groups—information security, IT operations, and development—collaborate to deliver highly available, cost-effective, and secure services. These organizations have moved beyond a focus on technology to address the core operational aspects of information security by building information security into key development and production processes. They have come to the realization that information security isn't just about technology; it's about process integration and managing people as well.

The Two Conflicting Goals Of IT

Although IT supports the business in many different ways, IT has two primary functions:

1. Developing new capabilities and functionality to achieve business objectives

2. Operating and maintaining existing IT services to safeguard business commitments

The first objective is typically owned by application development, and the second objective is typically owned by IT operations. To help both groups achieve their goals, information security and audit help verify that controls are properly designed and operating effectively.

Development objectives are primarily around delivering enhancements or additions to functionality that align with the changing needs of the business. Development is continually under pressure to increase agility to quickly respond to urgent business needs with fewer resources.

IT operations objectives are primarily around assuring stable, predictable, and secure IT services. IT operations is continually under pressure to improve service levels and reduce ongoing costs.

In this type of an environment, a core and chronic conflict between these two groups almost always develops. To respond to urgent business needs, development is pressured to do work and make changes faster. On the other hand, to provide a stable, secure and reliable IT service, IT operations is pressured to do work and make changes more slowly and carefully—or even make no changes at all (to reduce or avoid risk).

Resolving The Core, Chronic Conflict

Visible Ops Security describes how to resolve this core chronic conflict by enabling the business to simultaneously respond more quickly to urgent business needs and provide stable, secure, and predictable IT services.[3]

When information security sufficiently integrates into development, development can understand and implement information security requirements earlier and complete projects more quickly with less rework, resulting in faster time to market and lower costs. This results in development being better able to quickly respond to urgent business needs.

When information security sufficiently integrates into IT operations, IT operations can better manage risks, preventing incidents from occurring and quickly detecting and correcting incidents when they do occur (ideally before anyone is affected). By doing this, IT operations is better able to protect organizational commitments.

To make this a reality, information security must help the other groups recognize that this core, chronic conflict exists, and then work with them to resolve the conflict. The

---

[3] Dr. Eliyahu Goldratt, creator of the Theory of Constraints and author of *The Goal*, has written extensively on the theory and practice of identifying and resolving core, chronic conflicts.

goal is to have IT operations, development, and information security working together to achieve common objectives, as illustrated in Figure 1.

How do the authors know this is possible? Because high-performing IT operations and information security organizations have done it already.

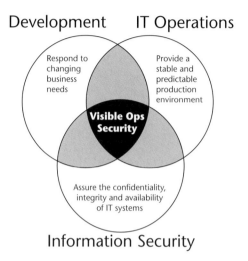

Figure 1: Visible Ops Security Focuses on the Point Where IT Operations, Development, and Information Security Objectives Overlap.

When Information Security Is Ineffective

The reality is that information security must work through other groups to achieve its objectives. Sustainable information security cannot be created by mandate or decree. It requires that information security work with other functional groups and integrate into their daily operations.

When this is not done effectively, people may use the following words to describe information security: *hysterical, irrelevant, bureaucratic, bottleneck, difficult to understand, not aligned with the business, immature, shrill, and perpetually focused on irrelevant technical minutiae.*[4]

These words very effectively describe the frustration that emerges when a control function (information security) appears to inhibit, without an understandable reason, the ability of other functions (development and IT operations) to achieve their objectives.

Attributes Of High-Performing Information Security Teams

Visible Ops Security helps information security professionals acquire high-performer attributes, which include:

- **Business aligned**—High-performing information security teams understand how security advances and protects business goals. Low performers focus on things the

[4] If the authors missed any adjectives, please mail us at authors@itpi.org.

business doesn't care about. They are obsessed with the improbable or irrelevant and are mired in technological minutia. Other groups may consider them hysterical.

- **Plugged in**—High-performing information security teams are integrated into the right functional groups even though they don't have direct operational responsibility. Low performers aren't present where the work is done and they're not helping the right people when they are needed. This reinforces the perception that information security is irrelevant.

- **Adding value**—High-performing information security teams provide value to business and IT process owners, and they know what they need from them in return. Low performers don't offer anything to advance the operational objectives of their colleagues, nor do they clearly articulate what they want people to do differently to meet information security requirements. Consequently, they are often viewed as incompetent.

- **Prioritized**—High-performing information security teams understand priorities and optimize the deployment of limited IT resources. Low performers insist on being involved, and then over commit resources causing project delays. Other groups see them as bottlenecks to meeting project and operational objectives.

- **People savvy**—High-performing information security teams leverage people and organizational skills to build effective working relationships with development and IT operations groups that make security sustainable. Low performers focus on technology risk, but cannot work through group dynamics to offer alternatives and find viable solutions. As a result, they frequently seem immature and they are ineffective in cross-functional group settings.

When information security teams have all these attributes, executives associate information security with *success*. Every attribute is essential. As Table 1 shows, if even one attribute is missing, those colorful adjectives appear.

Table 1: Missing attributes cause underperformance.

Exhibiting this attribute ...	causes information security to be perceived as...
Not being adequately business aligned	hysterical
Not being adequately plugged into processes	irrelevant
Not adequately adding value	incompetent
Not being adequately able to prioritize	a bottleneck
Not being adequately people savvy	immature

Integrating Information Security Into Daily Operations: Ending The Disconnect

Visible Ops Security is a prescriptive and phased approach that describes how to integrate information security into the daily operations of other functional groups in pragmatic and practical steps. It addresses the people and process issues, as well as the controls required to overcome them.

Readers do not need expertise in process improvement, information security, service development, IT operations, audit, or project management to read this book. Readers do not need extensive knowledge of process frameworks such as ITIL® (IT Infrastructure Library), or of control frameworks such as Control Objectives for Information and related Technology (COBIT) and ISO/IEC 27001 and 27002 (evolved from BS 7799/ISO 17799). These topics are introduced as they become necessary for implementing *Visible Ops Security*.

This book is intended to serve as a bridge for these process frameworks. It introduces the practices and language necessary to allow different functional groups to have a common view of the problem and a common approach to a solution.

For each process that information security needs to be integrating into, *Visible Ops Security* describes how we as information security will do the following:

- Understand the business and IT process inputs and outputs.
- Understand how we can help the process owners achieve their objectives.
- Understand how the process owners can help us achieve our security objectives.
- Be able to articulate what we want the process owners to do differently.
- Be able to measure how well our combined efforts are working.

The two toughest questions to answer are typically, "Where do I start?" and "Where do I go after that?" *Visible Ops Security* answers both. There is one caveat: To be successful, we must do the phases and steps in the prescribed sequence. In some cases, we may be able to do two phases in parallel, but we should never do the phases in reverse order. We will be starting with the production environment, and moving upstream, so order matters.

Phase 1: Stabilize The Patient And Get Plugged Into Production—In this phase, we start to gain meaningful situational awareness and integrate into daily IT operational processes. We integrate with change management, reduce access, and develop information security incident handling procedures that are integrated with the IT operations incident management process. Our goal is to gain visibility and begin to reduce risks in IT operations. This allows us to more quickly detect and correct information security incidents, reduce the likelihood of information security incidents, as well as help IT operations increase availability and reduce unplanned work.

Phase 2: Find Business Risks And Fix Fragile Artifacts—In this phase, we apply a top-down, risk-based approach to understand what matters most to the business, understand which IT services and systems are in scope, and then determine what IT controls are required to protect identified critical IT functionality. We then find and fix any IT control issues.

Phase 3: Implement Development And Release Controls—In this phase, our objective is to improve the quality of releases to ensure that information security standards are integrated into projects and builds. We do this by integrating into internal audit, project management, development, and release management. We also work with accounting and purchasing to increase our situational awareness and ensure that the controls we've built are working.

Phase 4: Continual Improvement—In this phase, we select and implement relevant measures to incorporate into organizational continuous process improvement efforts. We will look at both short-term and long-term effectiveness metrics.

Defining Terms Used In This Book

Because *Visible Ops Security* spans the domains of information security, IT operations, development, audit, compliance, and the business, we have to understand the terminology and all of the other functional groups, and make sure they understand ours. We use the following terms interchangeably, with our preferred term in bold.

Information security IT security Security Infosec	The functional group tasked with safeguarding organizational goals in the domain of information. The term "information security" is used over the other terms as our objectives and the risks that we are managing may extend beyond IT.
IT operations IT production Operations Production	The functional group responsible for the ongoing operations of IT services and ensuring that organizational commitments are met.
ITIL service support processes (v2) ITIL service transition and operations processes (v3)	Change, configuration, release, incident, and problem processes are described in the ITIL Service Support volume. These topics are covered in *The Visible Ops Handbook*. (ITIL v3 reorganized these processes into the Service Design, Service Transition and Service Operations books.) A best practice framework for IT. This book leverages various aspects of ITIL, but readers are not required to have prior detailed knowledge.
IT general control processes IT general controls Infrastructure controls	The category of controls used primarily by auditors to that apply "to all systems components, processes, and data for a given organization or systems environment. The controls include, but are not limited to: information security policy, administration, access, and authentication; separation of key IT functions; management of systems, acquisition and implementation; change management, backup; recovery; and business continuity."[5] Many of the IT general control processes are covered by ITIL. The term "IT general control processes" is used instead of "IT general controls" to emphasize that controls must be viewed as part of IT processes. After all, a basic premise is that we can have processes without controls, but it is impossible to have effective controls without process. Ed Hill asserts that "the term IT general controls reinforce the mistaken notion that IT controls exist outside of the context of IT processes, and that IT controls that don't actually relate to each other." In other words, we cannot reduce controls to individual controls. They must exist in the context of the IT service, the IT operational processes that support them, as well as with the other IT controls in place. COBIT is a control framework, defining 34 high-level control objectives, which are then broken down in 215 detailed control objectives.
Application controls	The category of controls within an application or automated within a business process that limit the risk of fraud or human error causing the application to perform in a manner other than designed. Examples include reasonableness checks, data edits, separation of business functions (e.g., transaction initiation versus authorization), balancing of processing totals, transaction logging, and error reporting.[6]
SDLC Software development life cycle Service development life cycle	The set of standards that define how services are to be created including requirements definition, programming standards, testing protocols, documentation, etc.

[5] Institute of Internal Auditors, "GTAG 1: Information Technology Controls", 2004.

[6] Adapted from Institute of Internal Auditors, "GTAG 1: Information Technology Controls", 2004.

Phase 1: Stabilize the Patient and Get Plugged into Production

What Are We Going to Do?

In this phase, our goal as information security practitioners is to gain situational awareness, insert information security into the IT operational environment[7] through the change management and access management processes, and then integrate the information security incident response procedures into the IT incident and problem management processes. By doing this, we will integrate information security into daily IT operations, to more effectively manage both information security and operational risks. This, in turn, lets us start building value for information security, IT operations, and the organization.

As a result, information security and IT operations will stop undoing each other's work and end friendly fire incidents. We will significantly reduce the amount of reactive work for both groups, freeing up resources to do more proactive and preventive work in the next phases.

Issues and Indicators

Visible Ops Security Phase 1 tackles the following issues:

Issue	Narrative Example
Inadequate situational awareness	I came into the information security job full of high hopes, but I started to realize that I was dropped into the desert, with no idea what direction I was supposed to start walking in. Worse, I didn't know how big the desert was, but I did know that I had no food or water.
	I also started to notice that everyone seemed to be avoiding me, often running in the opposite direction when they saw me.
Not plugged into relevant processes causes surprises and being steamrolled	Things happen to information security without warning. Last month, we found out about a high-visibility application upgrade two days before it was scheduled to go into production. The good news is that we got wind of it, and bullied our way into the project to do a security review. The bad news is that we found 17 very serious information security issues that needed to be fixed before rollout. The developers estimated that the fixes would delay deployment by four weeks and cost about a half-million dollars that weren't budgeted.
	The project team looked at the impact to the budget and delivery date, and then just blew us off and deployed anyway.
Information security ineffective as an afterthought	We couldn't believe they just deployed the application over our objections. I'm literally losing sleep at night because of the potential risk of loss of confidential information. I said, "Look, you can't put private health information out on the public Internet." They just don't seem to understand, and they all say I'm being hysterical, paranoid, and an obstacle.
	Management didn't even consider stopping the application deployment, and no one seems to care that they're potentially putting the entire organization at risk. Frankly, I think they're making all decisions above their pay grade.

[7] What ITIL v3 would consider the IT Service Operation environment

Issue	Narrative Example
Information security slowing everything down	To get the auditors off our backs, information security went through all of COBIT and ISO 27002:2005, and decided to implement 83 new controls for all of our major systems. It took almost a year to build all those flowcharts with the operational teams, and then build out the new procedures. That was painful, but not nearly as painful as having to live with these new processes.
	We are now moving slower than ever. We spend more time filling out forms and checking off checklists than performing real work. We hate it, but IT operations and development hate it even more. One of the application development VPs actually blamed information security for having to hire two full-time people that do nothing except expediting submitted change request forms.
Information security not plugged into production	Because everyone believes that information security is in the way of everything, people just go around us. We try to put controls in so that things don't get put into production without review and authorization, but IT operations just goes around our controls.
	We say "no" to something, but they do it anyway. We're constantly fighting with IT operations. There are days that information security and IT operations spend more time finger-pointing and undoing each other's work than actually getting planned work done.
Information security disrupts IT operations and IT operations gets in information security's way	We can't even do patching very well. We have a whole backlog of urgent patches that need to be deployed, but the IT operations people never seem to get around to them. We're almost eight months behind on patches now.
	And half the time, when we do get the patches in, I almost wish we hadn't. At the end of last year, we did a database patch that broke seven of our top business applications. We had to mobilize almost every DBA and developer, plus two vendors, to figure out why all the applications broke and get them running again.
	And who gets blamed? Not the IT operations staff or developers for not adequately testing it. Instead, all fingers pointed at information security for blowing up the servers. Does this seem fair?
Audit and regulatory compliance putting more pressure than ever	Now nobody bothers to get information security involved until there is some sort of audit finding, which causes everybody in IT to scramble. Last week, audit identified a significant weakness, and information security was left holding the bag, even though it was because some IT managers had ghost accounts and excessive developer access. The problem is these audit issues were jeopardizing the annual financial statements, and management wanted it resolved immediately. Literally, they gave us two days to get it done. It was end of quarter, and either we fixed it or we were history.
	We are now getting all sorts of attention we don't want, including the attention of two people from the board of directors. We've never had to interact with them before. No one is cooperating with me to resolve these issues, and I'm starting to feel genuinely isolated and afraid that we won't be able to preserve our commitments to this organization.
Information security breaches creating pressure	Audit issues aside, we know that bad things are happening all around us. We just don't know what we don't know, and the resulting information security risks to the organization are probably very huge. But we don't know exactly where they are lurking. So far, there hasn't been another major security breach like the one that got the last information security executive fired. This is not because things are secure. It's just that we've been lucky, and our luck is bound to run out soon.
Information security not adding value to the organization	Information security seems to have a reputation for not being team players, and being better at getting in the way than providing any real value. We not only feel unwelcome at meetings, but also it's getting to the point where I don't even want to attend the meetings anymore. We're holding the canteen out for everyone else, but no one wants to drink! How can you save the world when it doesn't want to be saved?
	It can't possibly be our fault that everyone reacts to information security this way, can it?

The steps in Phase 1 insert information security into IT operational processes, allowing us to:

- Influence daily IT operations by integrating information security into existing control points and approval processes.
- Provide value to IT operations so the IT operations staff will continue to want to work with information security.
- Reduce the amount of reactive work for IT operations and information security.

As we integrate into the change, access, incident, and problem management processes, we also significantly improve the effectiveness of how information security performs incident handling. By doing so, we become more effective at quickly detecting and recovering from information security incidents, specifically unauthorized access and unauthorized change.

Step 1: Gain Situational Awareness

> *"Enthusiasm without knowledge is like running in the dark. You might get there, but you might also get killed."*—UNKNOWN

In military parlance, there is a concept known as *situational awareness*. It is defined as "the ability to identify, process, and comprehend the critical elements of information about what is happening to the team with regard to the mission."[8]

Having situational awareness is especially relevant when information security is viewed as an obstacle, because IT operations will go to great lengths to not inform information security of what they are working on. Consequently, information security doesn't have a complete or accurate view of the current situation, and is, therefore, often surprised and unprepared.

In this step, we start building situational awareness so that we can better plan, execute, and respond. To have adequate situational awareness, we must know the following:

1. What senior management and the business wants from information security.

2. How the business units are organized and operate.

3. What the IT process and technology landscapes are.

4. What the high-level risk indicators from the past are.

Task 1: Find out what senior management and the business wants from information security

> *"Learning usually passes through three stages. In the beginning, you learn the right answers. In the second stage, you learn the right questions. In the third and final stage, you learn which questions are worth asking."*—UNKNOWN

We must understand management's intent from a business and an information security perspective. The business perspective provides the context that frames everything else. To gain this perspective, we need to have conversations with the senior business leaders whom information security serves. These conversations answer two important questions:

---

[8] http://www.dirauxwest.org/TCTF/situational_awareness5.htm

What are the business goals and what are the critical success factors that information security can help the organization achieve?

Ideally, overall business strategy and goals are neatly framed in a strategic planning document. If not, publicly traded companies often summarize their business strategy with a list of primary risks in the annual report to the shareholders. Regardless of the format of the document, it helps us understand where the business is going, and, at a minimum, ensures that information security is going in the same direction.

If we're going to determine what the business needs from information security, we must avoid philosophical discussions. Instead, we should identify key success factors that must be met to reach the overall business objectives. The following phrases encapsulate some key success factors that require information security:

- Avoid negative publicity. In other words, keep us off the front pages of the newspaper, unlike our competitor who left the front door open for the credit card data breach that resulted in headline news and three class-action lawsuits.

- Ensure that we comply with applicable laws, regulations, and standards such as Sarbanes-Oxley (SOX) Section 404, the Federal Information Security Management Act of 2002 (FISMA), and Payment Card Industry (PCI) Data Security Standard, and Basel II in Europe. Ensure that appropriate controls exist to support these various legal and regulatory requirements.

- Protect confidential information to safeguard personally identifiable information (PII),[9] trade secrets, intellectual property, financial reports, and other valuable corporate data. Ensure that appropriate information security controls exist to safeguard PII by controlling access, change, vulnerabilities, etc.

Task 2: Find out how the business units are organized and operate

> *"The leader of the past knew how to tell, the leader of the future will know how to ask."*—PETER DRUCKER

Next, we must identify the most important areas of the business—we have finite time and resources and must focus our efforts on what matters. There are several ways to do this. Often it can be as simple as reviewing the company financial income statements and identifying which business units have the most significant revenues and profits. Our goal is to know the names of the major organizational units and the key people in those units.

We must also interview management and understand the strategic direction of the organization, so that we don't miss any strategically important business units (e.g., units that are small now, but are vital to the company strategy).

Here is an example of the level of understanding that we are striving to obtain:

> *The enterprise is a $5 billion semiconductor company with two primary lines of business: chip fabrication and embedded software. These two business units contribute 50 percent and 30 percent of revenue, respectively. Because these two units represent the majority of revenue, we will focus on them.*

---

[9] What the PII acronym stands for varies: personally identifiable information, personal identity information, and so forth.

We know who leads each business unit, and we know the heads of the IT departments that support them. We have the organizational charts, so we have some idea of whom we need to talk to for various areas of responsibility.

We have learned from senior management and IT executives what worries them the most. We have formed some opinions on spheres of influence. We know who likes information security and who doesn't. We know who has budget and resources. And we know who can influence the people with these resources because they share common goals.

We know who in the business to contact in the event of a security incident. We have determined the key risks that the business cares about, and have added them to our situational awareness.

Task 3: What are the IT process and technology landscapes

Now we must discover the IT process and technology landscapes that enable the primary business areas we have identified. We will learn the specific technologies used in these businesses, the degree of reliance on the technology, who the IT process owners are, etc.

Continuing with our semiconductor company example, here's the level of understanding we want to achieve:

The mission-critical IT services that the chip fabrication business unit depends upon enable the following business processes: materials management, accounting, sales and order entry, customer service, and production control. The majority of these services are provided through the use of commercial off-the-shelf (COTS) software. Most run on UNIX® systems and Oracle® databases at a centralized data center located at company headquarters. Fabrication plants connect to the data center over the Internet or by leased OC-48 fiber lines.

For the embedded software division, we know that engineering and development are done at the company headquarters, and QA is outsourced to a vendor in Mumbai. The mission-critical IT services are source code control, automated QA tools, customer service, defect tracking, and network connectivity. Half of these services are developed internally. Defect tracking systems are managed by an outsourced vendor. The various IT services use virtually every major type of database, operating system and are seemingly managed by just as many different IT owners. Connectivity among offices is done entirely over the Internet.

We've learned about the frequency of IT service upgrades, which are a combination of ad hoc and monthly. We know who owns the IT change management process and we've identified the service owners from the development and IT operations perspectives.

At this point, we have a basic understanding of the IT entities. We don't know everything, but we know enough to understand which IT systems matter and why. What's more, we are starting to understand the people and process aspects for those systems. Just as important, we know which IT systems are not critical to the business, so we won't spend much time on those, lest we misuse our finite time, resources, and capital.

In Phase 2, we will drill down into the critical systems to understand more about legal and regulatory requirements as well as corresponding IT general control process requirements.

Task 4: Find the high-level risk indicators

In the absence of perfect knowledge, past performance can be a good predictor of future performance. Consequently, we can find problem areas by looking for red flags or indicators of past information security and control issues. To piece together this history for the IT entities identified above, we ask specific questions of internal audit, legal counsel, and the network operations center (NOC) staff that support them.

- What major information security incidents have occurred?
- What audit findings have there been?
- Are there any lawsuits around intellectual property? Were IT deficiencies the cause of the lawsuit or did IT hinder lawsuit discovery activities?
- What critical service outages or impairments have occurred? (We may also ask customers the same question.)
- What, if any, remediation has been undertaken for the above?

How far back should we go? Often, the answer is "about two years," as issues prior to this may no longer be relevant.

As we answer these questions, here's the level of understanding we want to gain:

> The chip fabrication business unit has experienced no information security incidents. However, at least one major outage per quarter occurs as a result of SAP® BASIS changes made to the financial modules. One time, an outage delayed the company SEC 10-Q financial report filings. There have been repeat audit findings around change and access controls. One of them resulted in a significant deficiency from the external auditor. Customer satisfaction with IT is low.

> For the embedded software business unit, customer satisfaction with IT is high. Audit, however, worries that contracts with the outsourced defect-tracking vendor in India fail to cover information security requirements for company data. Although IT operations has warned repeatedly that the network link between the United States and India is not encrypted, budget for the virtual private network (VPN) has remained on the backburner for the last three years.

Step 2: Integrate Into Change Management

In many ways, information security and change management have similar missions: Both groups are trying to manage risk. Information security needs change management to gain situational awareness of production changes and to influence decisions and outcomes. Even if we achieved the mythical "perfectly secure state," any change can quickly take us out of that secure state. One of the high-performing IT organizations studied in *The Visible Ops Handbook* observed that, "Enforcing our change management processes is critical, because we are always only one change away from being a low performer." Similarly, we know that we are always only "one change away from an information security incident that puts us on the front pages of the newspapers."

In this step, we embed information security into the change management process so that we can:

- Help assess the potential information security and operational impact of changes.
- Ensure that change requests comply with information security requirements, corporate policy, and industry standards.
- Recommend alternatives for risky changes instead of merely denying them.
- Request changes needed to address information security risks.

When we do these things, we align ourselves closely with the responsibilities of the change manager. We position ourselves to help the change manager enforce the integrity of the change management process by ensuring that all changes are properly authorized, and that unauthorized changes are detected and investigated appropriately.

Task 1: Get invited to change advisory board (CAB) meetings

"Inspection with the aim of finding the bad ones and throwing them out is too late, ineffective, costly. Quality comes not from inspection but from improvement of the process."—W. EDWARDS DEMING

The best place to get an ongoing picture of changes, major projects, and other work in progress is the regularly scheduled change advisory board (CAB) meetings. CAB meetings are the forum for assessing the risks of proposed changes, approving or denying change requests, reviewing the status of changes being planned, agreeing on implementation schedules, and reviewing the success of implemented changes[10].

Information security often is not invited to participate in the CAB. Sometimes this is just an oversight. Other times, information security people find themselves "uninvited" because they are perceived as saying "no" too often without offering viable alternatives. Consequently, they are seen as roadblocks and too painful to interact with.

In either case, we need to make friends with the change manager and get ourselves invited to the CAB meetings. So we're going to pick up the phone and call the change manager. (This, by the way, is the first of many phone calls we will make as we progress through the Visible Ops Security methodology.) We introduce ourselves and explain the purpose of our call. Here's how the conversation might go:

"I bet you're tired of rework and last-minute panic efforts that keep cropping up because information security requirements are thrown in at the last minute instead of being considered early in the change and release planning processes. Let me tell you, I sure am frustrated with this, and let's not even get started on how this affects our audits. We are all spending so much time preparing for and being audited, that we don't have time to make any progress doing our real jobs. Would you be interested in working together to tackle these problems?"

When talking with the change manager, we emphasize the value we can bring through participation in the CAB, including:

---

[10] If there is no change management process in the IT organization, and, therefore, no change manager and no CAB meetings, then we must establish rudimentary change management processes and participate in them. *The Visible Ops Handbook* addresses how to do this.

- Reducing rework and last-minute panic work by ensuring that information security requirements are considered early in the planning process.

- Safeguarding the functional area objectives of the CAB stakeholders—for example, in changes related to human resources (HR) systems, we help ensure adherence to internal privacy policies and regulatory guidelines.

- Protecting confidential information, including customer and employee data.

- Bridging the change process between IT management and auditors—both internal and external.

- Reducing the workload before and during audits, as well as reducing the likelihood and severity of audit findings.

Our phone conversation will suggest to the change manager that we can be a valuable asset to the CAB. Now we have to deliver on that promise. When we attend CAB meetings, we must ask thoughtful questions, such as:

- What are the relevant information security or compliance requirements for the IT assets affected by the request for change (RFC)? Here are some examples: The enterprise resource planning (ERP) system must meet financial reporting internal control objectives. Point-of-sale devices must meet PCI compliance requirements. Firewall configuration rules are involved in all of the above.

- Can these proposed changes jeopardize those internal control objectives, and if so, how? In other words, if these changes are made, how will they affect existing internal controls?

- What activities are necessary in the change management process to manage the risks associated with this RFC, and what evidence is necessary to substantiate completion of those activities?[11] The critical steps for change management are authorization, documentation, testing, and substantiation or verification.[12] Furthermore, we want documentation to show that the implemented change is operating as planned.

- Have all required security tests been performed? Of course, this implies that information security policies have been documented and approved by management.

Note that the third bullet is about activities necessary to fulfill and substantiate control requirements. This is one of the primary reasons we want to be invited to CAB meetings, which is to establish and reinforce that preventive controls are implemented through policies, procedures, and enforced through the change management process. It is less expensive and easier to prevent issues than to correct them after the fact.

Attending the CAB meetings significantly increases our situational awareness, but we must also work to continually get involved as early as possible in the planning of upcoming changes. In Phase 3, we will formalize how to integrate with development and project management.

In this task, we have focused on preventive change controls. In the remaining tasks of this step, we focus on the corresponding detective change controls and deterrents.

---

[11] Readers with audit experience will note that the word "activities" actually refers to "control objectives."

[12] The verification that the change went in as planned could be part of what ITIL v3 identifies as a post implementation review.

Task 2: Build and electrify the fence

"If standards and regulations are not revised in six months, it is proof that no one is seriously using them."—KAORU ISHIKAWA

Information security hinges on the effectiveness of the change management process. As a result, we need to implement a detective control to verify compliance and take decisive action when the process is not followed.

Having a detective change control enables us to determine:

- Precisely what changed in the IT environment.
- Whether changes were properly authorized.
- Whether the change conformed to required standards.
- Relevant forensics data in case we have to conduct an information security investigation.

Detective change controls can be manual, automated, or semi-automated. Given the complexity and volume of changes, automated methods are almost always preferable. To illustrate this, here are the methods for substantiating that no unauthorized changes have occurred:

- **Manual**—There are at least two manual methods. One method is to review outage records. If root cause analysis is performed, determine whether unauthorized changes were the cause. The other method is to talk to customers to determine if unauthorized changes were made.

- **Semi-automated**—We can devise some solutions even if we don't have change monitoring in place without having to resort to completely manual methods. This might include comparing the current systems to tape backups or Norton Ghost® images to generate a listing of file changes. This can then be reconciled to authorized RFCs.

- **Automated**—We have some technology in place, such as Tripwire®, that is monitoring the configurations and settings of IT infrastructure that matter, and then we have someone reconciling those changes to an authorized RFC. We can take this one step further, not only reconciling to the change management process, but also reconciling to the test systems to show that the deployed changes match only the authorized and tested changes.

An efficient detective control is repeatable and cost effective. Neither the manual or semi-automated methods meet these criteria. The authors have found that even small IT organizations quickly discover that manual and semi-automated methods are too costly and error prone to be sustainable over time. When there is complexity, automated methods are necessary. Given the rate of change in services and the need for timely alerting, the only effective approach is to implement an automated control that generates reports on detected changes at least on a daily basis.

For these reasons, and those outlined in the original *Visible Ops Handbook*, our goal is to have automated detective controls in place and integrated into daily operations, so that when there are outages, or when auditors request substantiation, we can quickly answer the question "what has changed?" without having to resort to firefighting and forensic archaeology during outages.

By reconciling detected changes to authorized RFCs, we support the assertion that all changes have been authorized. By reconciling detected changes to changes on the test systems, we support the assertion that no unauthorized changes have been made between testing and production release.

Most auditors will be impressed by our ability to demonstrate that we are aware of all the changes that were made to a particular system and can link them to authorized RFCs. Just imagine their amazement when IT management can actually substantiate its claims without archaeology, last minute documentation quests, and hordes of auditors showing up with suitcases!

Task 3: Ensure tone from the top and define the consequences

"A business will have good security if its corporate culture is correct. That depends on one thing: tone at the top. There will be no grassroots effort to overwhelm corporate neglect." — WILLIAM MALIK, GARTNER

In this task, we influence top management to set the proper tone with respect to information security. Auditors use the term *tone from the top* to express the fact that words and actions from the boardroom on down set the tone for the behavior of everyone in the enterprise. In our case, the tone from the top we're looking for is this: The only acceptable number of unauthorized changes is zero and senior executives will not tolerate people circumventing the change management process.

It may be as simple as having the Chief Information Officer (CIO) or VP of Operations send out an e-mail message that says:

"Team, no matter how we did things before, the only acceptable number of unauthorized changes is zero. Unauthorized change jeopardizes every objective we care about, including availability, compliance, information security, and project delivery. So this policy applies equally to IT personnel and those in the other organizational units, such as marketing and sales. To enforce this policy, we are putting monitoring controls in place. When we find people who intentionally violate this policy, we are prepared to take decisive action to address this unacceptable behavior."

This simple declaration, however, is not sufficient. Management must back it up with quick and decisive action when anyone knowingly makes unauthorized changes. The course of action should be defined with HR to ensure that all cases are dealt with properly. Potential action can take any of several forms:

- **Three strikes and you're out**—IT people who consistently fail to follow the process are put in a role that does not allow them to make any changes. This may mean taking away production access, a transfer to another department, or demotion.

- **Wall of shame**—Management posts a list of repeat offenders in a highly visible location.

- **Being sent home for the day**—Anyone who makes an unauthorized change is relieved of duties for the day to give them time to ponder what is more important: shortcutting process or being trusted to behave responsibly.

- **Individual "compassionate coaching" by the VP of Operations**—IT operations executives are not known for being soft-spoken. That's because the buck usually stops at their desk and their jobs could be on the line when changes cause major incidents or outages. So the tone of their "coaching" usually proves effective.

- **Escalation with management**—This may be appropriate when certain units are found guilty of consistently circumventing the official change process. For example, suppose the marketing department is consistently expediting IT changes over the weekend to preserve date commitments for the following Monday, forcing IT to do heroics and potentially cut corners that may not be acceptable to the business if all the risks were known. When this occurs, as information security professionals, we must make the cause-effect relationship of these actions known and its consequences understood, and prevent it from happening in the future.

For some of these actions, information security and IT may have to work closely with HR to establish the appropriateness of the disciplinary policies.

There may be some overlap between the responsibilities of the change manager and information security roles around investigating unauthorized change. An example of how responsibilities could be divided between the two groups is shown below:

Source of Change	Action Required	Owner
Authorized person, authorized change	None – process is in compliance.	Change manager
Authorized person, unauthorized change (well intended, erroneous, or malicious).	Change should be rolled back and root cause investigated. Information security reviews and starts formal investigation if necessary.	Change manager, if there is no malicious intent suspected Information security, if malicious intent is suspected
Unauthorized person, unauthorized change	Information security starts investigation and must immediately understand what changed; returns services to trusted states with the assistance of IT operations	Information security

Task 4: Substantiate that the electric fence is working

"Trust, but verify."—DAMON RUNYON

During an audit, if we cannot support the assertion that no unauthorized changes were made, then the integrity of the IT services and systems becomes unknown. This weakness in the change management process forces the search for compensating controls to regain confidence that the IT services and systems are operating as designed.

To substantiate compliance with change management for all services in scope, we need to prepare in advance of the audit evidence of the following:

- Change requests and their approvals
- Changes detected on all relevant IT systems

- Reconciliations of detected changes to approved changed requests
- Any corrective actions undertaken for unauthorized changes

Detective change controls make good business sense. A 2007 IT Process Institute study shows that a process culture and monitoring configurations are significant predictors of high levels of IT performance and information security's ability to automatically detect and quickly recover from information security breaches.[13]

To make sure that this evidence is sufficient for an upcoming audit, we will call the internal auditor and confirm the evidence requirements and the validity of our approach.[14]

Task 5: Look for red flags

"[As auditors,] the top leading indicators of risk when we look at an IT operation are poor service levels and unusual rates of changes."—BILL PHILHOWER

In this task, we want to scan the forest looking for smoke because where there's smoke, there's fire. Or, as auditors would say, we are looking for red flags and indicators that people are circumventing the change management process.

To quickly determine the health of the change management process, we merely have to look for firefighting and unplanned work, as well as any availability problems. Why? Because we know that the largest threats to availability are improperly planned and executed changes.

According to industry estimates, 80 percent of all outages are change related. For availability-challenged services, we can safely determine that changes are not being effectively managed (i.e., reviewed, tested, authorized, and enforced) by asking questions such as:

- Do change requests have effective risk assessment before implementation?
- Are planned changes being effectively reviewed by knowledgeable parties?
- Are planned changes being communicated?
- Are changes being adequately tested before release to production?
- Are all production changes automatically detected and reconciled to authorized change?
- Are unauthorized changes decisively acted upon?
- Is root cause analysis done on failed changes to prevent them from happening in the future?

To focus our attention, we will analyze major outages during a given period (e.g., the previous week) and determine whether change was a causal factor. If it was, then we must find out whether that change was approved and scheduled for that time. If the change was not approved, we must initiate an investigation into the unauthorized change.

---

[13] "IT Process Institute Change, Configuration, and Release Study" 2007.
[14] For a more complete set of prescriptive guidance on how to prepare for an IT audit, see Appendix A of *The Visible Ops Handbook*.

We should also look at what percentage of change requests are emergency changes. As a general rule, emergency changes should not constitute more than five to eight percent of all changes. When there is a sufficiently high rate of emergency change (e.g., 25 percent), we can safely assume that the organization doesn't have a functional change management process, and is certainly not managing risk. In these situations, typically IT and business teams have learned that they can get changes approved faster by falsely declaring an emergency. Change management has inadvertently created an "express lane" for unsafe changes!

When we find these red flags and indicators, we will actively publicize them to focus management attention on them and to fix the change management process. This improves the information security control environment, and also adds value to IT operations and the business by increasing availability.

Task 6: Address failed changes

> *"Experience comes from what we have done. Wisdom comes from what we have done badly."*—THEODORE LEVITT, HARVARD BUSINESS SCHOOL

We must continually focus attention on failed changes and process exceptions, and take steps to prevent future failures. Why? Change management processes that do not reduce the likelihood of change failures are not managing risk. Information security can help by identifying problems and proposing constructive solutions.

Here are some examples of analysis that we would want to foster in a CAB meeting:

> *"Last week, we had a two-hour unplanned outage on the ERP system due to an unauthorized change to the database server. The database manager has talked with the DBA, but I'm not convinced that any corrective action was taken. I don't believe the manager even got a verbal commitment from the DBA to never do it again. I'm going to talk to the VP of Operations and the database manager to tell them why violations of the change management policy cannot be tolerated."*

> *"Last week, another outage on the customer Web site meant that order entry was down for 30 minutes. We engaged with problem management and have not yet established any root cause. There is some finger-pointing regarding the cause. Information security thinks it was due to an application change. IT operations thinks it was a firewall rule change. At this point, I think it's all rumor and hearsay. I will have an update by next week, but until we have better monitoring and controls, we may never get beyond this he-said/she-said situation. If outages here continue, we need to figure out what is really happening, and do it before senior management asks us tougher questions. If we're serious, we have to put the appropriate controls in place so we can manage by fact, instead of by rumor."*

> *"For the third week in a row, we had an emergency change order submitted on a Friday for a change to be made on Saturday. While the team got the application working by Monday morning, it took the entire weekend to make the change operational. What scares me is that we were testing in production because QA never even got to test this release. Someone needs to sit down with this business unit and figure out why they have so many emergency changes. Is it a product launch? Is it some activity related to mergers and acquisitions? Or is it simply failure to*

plan? Whatever the case, they are putting IT operations and the business at risk by abusing the emergency change procedure and bypassing full testing."

These types of comments help the CAB proactively manage risk and improve the quality of decisions. As a result, they enhance the system of controls to better protect information security objectives and business goals.

We also want to focus attention on managing risk and process improvement by suggesting post-implementation reviews of all changes, especially large or complex changes. As part of the review, the CAB would answer the following questions about each change:

- Was it completed successfully?
- If not, what was the root cause of the failure?
- Was it due to poor planning or human error?
- How could the process have been improved?

Step 3: Reduce And Control Access

"No institution can possibly survive if it needs geniuses or supermen to manage it. It must be organized in such a way as to be able to get along under a leadership composed of average human beings."—PETER DRUCKER

In the typical IT organization, many staff will often have more production access than they need to do their jobs. Excessive access[15] creates the potential risk for people to make uncontrolled changes to critical systems. This not only exposes IT systems to human error that can disrupt service, but also creates unnecessary vulnerabilities for malicious and criminal acts that jeopardize the organization. Here are a few examples:

Example 1: A developer has excessive access to a production system's options and can change the number of financial reporting periods. She inadvertently changes the number from 12 to 13 and the system converts all the data. The next morning, the financial numbers no longer match expected values, and the organization can no longer create financial statements. No one can figure out what happened for a day. After firefighting, IT has to restore the data from backup tape.

Example 2: A user with privileged access on a UNIX system tries to help by changing the permissions on all the application files. He inadvertently goes into the wrong directory when doing the recursive change group (chgrp) command. The system stops running. The environment was so dynamic that backup tapes would have lost significant amounts of data. It takes a full day of the most senior technical person's time to rectify the problem. As a result, the internationalization project behind a key strategic initiative was delayed.[16]

Example 3: A DBA has privileges to add, remove, and modify financial transactions, as well as add, remove, and modify user accounts. He creates an account, grants privileges, adds a transaction to perform a check run, and writes a $1 million

---

[15] In this book, we will use the term "access" to denote both access and privilege. We are concerned with removing excesses in both.

[16] One of the authors of this book was the enthusiastic helper in this example.

check to himself. He executes the check run, and then removes all traces of the user account and the transaction.

In this step, we take action to prevent these risks, whether they are malicious or simply the result of human error. We do this by reducing access wherever possible and ensuring that some form of effective access control exists.

Reducing access makes good business sense. A 2007 IT Process Institute study shows that the ability to grant appropriate system access based on well-defined roles and responsibilities is a significant predictor of high levels of IT performance. It's also one of the most significant indicators of information security's ability to automatically detect and quickly recover from security breaches.[17]

Task 1: Reduce unnecessary access

The Visible Ops Handbook gave simple guidance around access:

> *"Reduce or eliminate access: Clear everyone away from the asset unless they are formally authorized to make changes. Because these assets have low change success rates, we must reduce the number of times the dice are rolled."*

Only personnel who are formally authorized should have access (regardless of whether they are current employees, contractors, business partners, or customers, etc.). Access should be based on a business need.

We start by removing developer access to all production services wherever possible, including applications, databases, operating systems, networking devices, and data. IT Process Institute studies show that 74 percent of high-performing IT organizations deny developer access to production systems.[18] This action delivers many benefits, including forcing the creation of an end-to-end development-to-release life cycle with appropriate handoff points, formalizing segregation of duties, and reducing the temptation to make unauthorized changes to production systems.

Next, we look at accounts with privileged access (e.g., Unix root, Windows enterprise and group administrators, AS/400 qsecofr accounts, and information security administrators). All personnel with privileged access must have formal approval and a genuine business need. For each of these accounts, there should be on file a request for access with the signature of an authorized manager.

If there isn't an existing procedure that has created a list of approved administrators, we still start by reducing the number of administrators with privileged access to as few as possible. This number will vary and we will need input from management. However, we know that 25 are too many (i.e., "everybody has root"), and one is too few (i.e., "only one person has root, and if she is hit by a bus, then no one can get root.").

We will focus on the most important business processes and IT services, work with management to figure out who should have administrative privileges, generate the formal approval documentation, and revoke the rest.

---

[17] "IT Process Institute Change, Configuration, and Release Study" 2007.
[18] Ibid.

Task 2: Establish an account management process[19]

Now that we have reduced access, we will replace the informal access request process (e.g., water cooler or hallway drive-by conversations) with a documented request process that includes proper approvals. A well-defined process to add, change, and revoke access is required for effective and secure account management.

Our goal is to define and implement a process to grant system access based on a user's business role and responsibilities. To do this, we must ensure that there is a formal business owner for each service who can review and approve access requests on the basis of business need. (The reason for this is that the business has a far better understanding of business need and people's roles than information security. For example, should Trent who works for the controller really have production access to the Kumquat Sasquatch IV 3.4 financial application only on Friday afternoons? The controller knows the answer far better than information security does.).

Next, we can help with the design of a standard user access request form that the business owners use. Once the user access request form is approved and signed by the business owner, a designated information security/system administrator creates or grants the identified access and signs and dates the request indicating that the work has been performed.

Because this is when the account creation work is done, we should also list all access control standards on this form, such as password complexity rules, password aging, and access management reports.

Task 3: Eliminate ghost accounts

Next, we will address the need for immediate removal of accounts when people leave the organization. In addition to this preventive policy control, we also need detective controls that review HR and payroll lists of terminated employees and contractors, and ensure that these people no longer have access to IT services.

Accounts that shouldn't be left active but remain on a system (e.g., the employee was terminated or the service is no longer used) are often called ghost accounts. Ghost accounts are vulnerabilities that can potentially be exploited, and are, therefore, the subject of audits.

We will build preventive and detective controls to eliminate these accounts. For preventive controls, we must work with HR to ensure that termination of IT access rights is included as a part of the company's dismissal checklist and termination workflow. In other words, we will make sure that access rights are revoked at the same time company ID cards, corporate credit cards, building keys, and other company property are collected, if not sooner. In the case of involuntary terminations, access rights should be revoked at the same time that the person is given notice to prevent malicious acts.

(We recommend that user accounts be disabled, not deleted. Many war stories describe how deleting user accounts can have unexpected and disastrous consequences, such as violating referential integrity, deleting historical log data, and so forth. Accounts can be immediately disabled, and later deleted, after the required investigation is completed.)

[19] For further reference, ITIL v3 now defines an access management process in the Service Operation volume.

We must also build the detective control by reviewing termination reports from HR and payroll. A regular report from each department shows us which employees have resigned, retired, or been terminated. We need reports from both departments because, in some organizations, one department or the other might not know of terminations right away. HR and payroll often live in different parts of the organization and report to different people. They may not talk to each other on a regular basis. We mitigate this risk by closing the loop with both departments.

We must make sure that during some defined time interval, someone is verifying on the IT systems that all relevant accounts are disabled. The same is true for contractor accounts. We must verify their status with the appropriate internal groups responsible for managing them. Any detected ghost accounts should trigger some corrective action. In situations where accounts weren't properly handled, the root cause should be investigated and the process improved.

There is one more loophole that we need to handle, which is the employee transfer process. We must implement similar controls in the employee transfer process as in the employee termination process. From a bookkeeping and organizational perspective, this is more challenging. Here's an example.

> *An accounts payable clerk transfers to purchasing. Initially, he continues to perform his accounts payable job while the organization finds and trains a replacement. To do this, he needs user accounts in both departments. This situation violates sound segregation-of-duties practices. The clerk could create a purchase order, receive against it, and state that payment is due. This exposes the business to the risk of human error and fraud that can have serious consequences.*

An employee transfer process can mitigate this type of risk. The process might specify a fixed period of time for revoking permissions—say 30 days. Ideally, the employee's manager would notify information security when the old permissions can be revoked. If the manager does not notify information security within the defined timeframe, information security reassesses permissions and either revokes them or extends them for an additional specified period. Reassessments are done regularly until the access is revoked.

As with terminations, we need a detective control. We need to obtain reports from HR and payroll that list all transferred employees. The lists should be compared to access change requests to determine whether access levels have appropriately changed or if further investigation is required. In situations where accounts weren't properly handled, the root cause should be investigated and the process improved.

Task 4: Re-accredit accounts routinely

Re-accreditation is our failsafe detective control to ensure that only the correct accounts are active and that each account has appropriate access permissions. Periodic re-accreditation is vital because account permissions may drift out of compliance over time. Re-accreditation also can help detect unauthorized accounts or other malicious activity such as excess privileges.

Re-accreditation involves management review of user accounts for each service. The business management who approves user requests must confirm that current privileges are accurate, and if not, specifies the corrective action. These reviews should occur at least annually and more frequently when drift is known to be a problem. For systems with thousands of users, the business owner may delegate the responsibility to review and approve existing accounts.

We must ensure that the business owner signs and dates this report. The appropriate parties in information security and/or IT operations would then implement corrections.

Again, if we find that the re-accreditation exercise shows that drift is occurring, we need to ask why. An authorized manager should review requested corrections and research the root cause to improve the process.

Step 4: Codify Information Security Incident Handling Procedures And Modify First Response

In the typical IT organization, the time when IT operations and information security have the most problems working together is during major incidents when stress levels are high. Often, it is not clear if a given problem is a genuine security breach or just another major outage. Problems include figuring out who did what to whom, who is responsible, and how to escalate appropriately without escalating to everybody.

Examples of things going wrong include:

- Information security is the last to find out when security breaches occur, and loses the ability to do quick damage containment and recovery. (e.g., "What do you mean you knew that someone was doing a database query every Friday and sending all these credit numbers through an SSH tunnel to Trinidad/Tobago?")
- Information security is often blamed for outages, especially around firewall rule changes. (e.g., "The EDI upload failed over the weekend. Everyone is sure that it was because of a firewall rule change.")
- Information security gets brought into every incident, although most of them are not security-related. The only thing worse than this is not being brought into every incident. (e.g., "I'm tired of being brought into conference calls on Saturday mornings at 2 am, but at least I'm aware of the latest catastrophes, most of which have some grave security implications.")
- IT operations does not escalate appropriately and mobilizes too many people too soon, pulling scarce IT resources away from planned work and activities, and prolonging repair times. (For example, "IT operations declared a Severity 1 outage, and mobilized everybody, including information security. We spent the first 30 minutes blaming each other for who caused the outage. We finally discovered that it was a single Active Directory change, and that no one else really needed to have been tied up on that five-hour conference call.")

In this step, our goal is to integrate information security into the IT operations resolution processes to ensure that information security is brought in appropriately only when needed. We will also define how to declare information security incidents, so that they may be resolved efficiently and effectively.

One difficulty is the unfortunate terminology collision between the ITIL definition of *incident management* and the information security concept of *incident handling*. For the purposes of implementing this step, we will use the following definitions that should satisfy both groups' needs:

In ITIL parlance, an incident is any deviation from normal operations. The incident management process is the route by which customers, users, and IT report deviations from normal operations or events that may threaten operations. In other words, when we see something that is outside the normal operating profiles of a service, we declare an incident. When a major incident occurs, a problem management ticket may be opened and team assembled to identify root cause. These are both situations that may warrant information security involvement.

By definition, almost any situation warranting the involvement of information security is an incident. Ideally, users should have a single point of contact with IT (via the ITIL service desk), regardless of whether the issue is related to IT operations or information security. Those incidents that are information security-related will trigger our formal information security incident handling procedures for investigation.

Our goal is to codify with the business and IT operations how information security incidents should be declared and managed. Ideally, this will be through the existing IT operations incident management system, so we can leverage all of the existing operational bookkeeping and configuration management information, as well escalation procedures, reporting, etc.

Task 1: Define when and how to engage information security

We start by building a relationship with the people in charge of incident and problem resolution. Just as we did with the change manager, we pick up the phone and call, introduce ourselves, and explain the purpose of our call. The conversation might go like this:

> *"I bet you're tired of having your staff spend time resolving incidents only to find out that information security had a quick answer. Or, I bet you're tired of never having access to information security people when you need them, or you see information security people hovering around when you don't need them.*
>
> *I'd like to fix this, too. Would you like to meet to create some general guidelines, codify some procedures, and identify what's information security relevant ahead of time, so we can quickly identify events that have security implications and mobilize information security appropriately?"*

When we meet with the incident and problem managers, we're prepared with examples of generalized rules such as the following:

- If the origin of the incident or problem is external to the organization, contact information security. (e.g., a phishing attack from Asia)
- If the incident or problem involves information security support services, contact information security. (e.g., firewalls, IDS/IPS, event correlation, or log servers)

- If the incident or problem deals with the loss of money, or confidential or proprietary information, let information security know immediately. (e.g., customer records, financial systems with suspicious balances, or bank transfers)

- If the incident or problem seems security-related, contact information security because many information security incidents are discovered by someone noticing something out of the ordinary. (e.g., "That's funny. Why are all the transaction monitors turned off and log feeds disabled?" "Why do we have stored procedures appearing and disappearing every Sunday morning?" "Why did the root password change, because all the database logins are not authenticating?")

- If employees have any concerns about an issue that may be security-related, they should be able to contact information security directly—even outside of standard business hours. We can use an awareness campaign to ensure that staff knows how to reach us. (However, in these scenarios, we then become responsible to record the interaction in the incident management system so it can be tracked, just like any other incident. An ITIL principle is that if it is important enough for a user to contact us, then it is important enough for us to record it.)

We work with the manager to establish information security triage procedures. The output of this activity will be integrated into the existing flowcharts and scripts that the service desk uses when talking with users.

Our goal is to make sure that the service desk, which often functions as the first level of incident management, captures the appropriate information that will allow us to establish whether an incident is information security-related as early in the incident management process as possible (e.g., on the first call within the first two minutes), and that service desk agents are capturing the relevant information necessary for rapid resolution (e.g., who, what, when, where, and contact information). This information must be routed to information security as quickly as possible.

We need to be realistic about how much we can script these interactions. The risk is that we may overly structure them, causing them to miss genuine information security incidents and taking away the ability of information security practitioners to use their own judgment. We do, however, script normal information security incidents, such as phishing at a bank, so people know how to handle and escalate these issues properly. Unless information security staff is answering the phones at the service desk (usually not realistic), then information security must arm the service desk with the right questions to ask to route information security issues appropriately.

Formalizing the information security incident response into the incident management process also solves the problem of ensuring that everyone knows how to engage information security. By clarifying how to escalate tickets to information security, we avoid the risks of urgent incidents being lost, not knowing whom to call, poor communications, and so forth.

Task 2: Confirm scope of detective change controls

A key question that information security must immediately answer for two reasons is "What changed?" The first reason is enable IT operations to determine whether change is a causal factor in an outage. The second reason is to enable information security to understand during an information security incident what changed, who made the change, and when the change was made to determine the correct course of action.

The Visible Ops Handbook described the need to have change information readily available during the resolution processes. In the handbook it was called "Modify First Response." There are two reasons we need to quickly understand what changed. First, we must determine if we are dealing with information security incident based on what changed. Second, to take effective and efficient corrective action we must also understand what changed.

In this task we must confirm that detective controls are in place and monitoring information security-relevant data, files, settings, firewalls, etc., in addition to what IT operations monitors. This is to ensure that information security can effectively participate in the resolution processes and that the necessary data is captured for information security incident handling, including forensics.

Task 3: Formalize information security incident response

The wrong time to think about how to handle emergencies is in the middle of a crisis. So, we need to think through and document how information security should be integrated with the rest of the organization. By doing this, we will formalize how IT operations hands information security the ball (through incidents and problems) in information security-relevant situations. And because we've made a big fuss over being relevant and needing to be involved, the worst thing we can do is fumble the ball the first time an incident or problem is handed to us.

We must now show that we're capable of carrying the ball by documenting in advance what we're going to do. And if the incident is determined not to be information security-related, we can gracefully release control and participate as needed.

Information security-relevant incidents must trigger some type of immediate information security investigation procedures regardless of the time of day or night. After all, management expects to have information security all the time, not just during business hours. That means information security has to provide 24x7 coverage—either through round-the-clock presence or through an established procedure for calling information security during off-hours.

With that in mind, here are critical elements of an information security response plan:

- A procedure that describes how the service desk should notify information security.
- Information security incident response procedures that document the step-by-step instructions with inputs, outputs, and decision criteria.
- Incident categorization that differentiates the types of information security incidents.
- The minimum set of activities required to resolve each category of information security incident.
- Roles and responsibilities of information security and IT operations staff.

- Defined escalation path for each incident category, defining the procedures and authority to act (such as, information security having the authority to take control of IT operations and turn systems off if necessary).
- Regulatory and contractual obligations that define requirements for reporting and response.
- Communications plan that defines how to engage key stakeholders in the business including marketing, legal, and HR for specific communications during and after information security incidents. (This should include their after hours contact information and backup personnel.)

The Spectrum Of Situational Awareness And Information Security Integration

As we increase our situational awareness and integration into daily IT operations, we reduce the level of reactiveness of how we respond to potential security threats. The following two examples show how responses evolve as the level of awareness of the environment increases.

Example 1: Abuse report from an external source:

"Hey, someone is on the phone from a bank, claiming that someone is attacking their servers from an IP address in our network. What's going on?"

Denial: *"That IP address doesn't look like one of ours. It's inconceivable that someone in our network is attacking them! Close the incident."*

Bewildered: *"That IP address hasn't been allocated to anyone inside the company. Maybe it's a hacker who infiltrated our network. Who should we contact to do more instrumentation? E-mail all the IT managers and see who is using that IP range, and tell them I need a response in 30 minutes!"*

Basic Awareness: *"The IP address is used by sales operations. Uh, oh. Isn't that where our sensitive customer data is that could be leaking out? Who in IT operations do I need to call to declare an information security incident in progress?"*

Service Awareness: *"That's coming from one of the sales operations servers, and probably the one that uploads data to suppliers. Here's the contact information of the responsible manager. Let's get her on the phone immediately to get to the bottom of this."*

Activity Awareness: *"I see that this is the sales operations server that does supplier order uploads. And I also see that they had a changed scheduled for today to modify the ordering upload frequency. I wonder if this is a genuine information security incident or some side effect of the change?"*

Situational Awareness: *"Ah, I see that the supplier upload server change may have accidentally changed the upload frequency from once per day to once per second. Open up a Severity 1 incident and request an emergency rollback of the change to the prior state to halt the unintended denial of service to one of our suppliers. I need some sort of status report in 30 minutes, because I owe this bank more information about the corrective actions we are taking."*

Example #2: An intrusion detection system (IDS) generates alerts:

> *"We may have a real problem. Someone just told me that we just had a trading service fail and that happens to have occurred at the same time all our intrusion detection systems started alerting. What is going on?"*

> **Denial:** *"The intrusion detection systems are always alerting all the time. Well, it's only one IDS. If it were a real attack, all IDS sensors would alert at the same time. Don't worry about it. Close the incident."*

> **Bewildered:** *"What systems are they attacking? Send e-mails out to the server and network teams and find out what systems are on that subnet, which servers are being hit and where they are located."*

> **Basic Awareness:** *"Those are the servers located in the Chicago data center that are tied to the Board of Trade. I'll contact that data center and find out what is going on. Hey, does anyone have the after-hours phone number of that IT operations group?"*

> **Service Awareness:** *"Those are the 20 Linux servers that are in the Chicago data center tied to the Board of Trade by a T1 going through router NWR00023 and firewall FW10112. Contact their IT owners and find out what is going on."*

> **Activity Awareness:** *"That's odd. We scanned for changes on the systems supporting the IT service, and found that someone changed the password of the database administrator login. Maybe this is what caused the failure. Who was authorized to change the password for the database administrator account?"*

> **Situational Awareness:** *"At 1:33am local time a port scan was executed on the private network from internal IP 192.168.1.101 and detected by the IDS9989A unit. At 2:05am local time, the service account "SysBackup123" changed the database administrator account on database servers "DB1156A" and "DB1156B". Documentation confirms that service account is for executing backups only and should not have been used to modify accounts. Furthermore, there are no change requests open to change the database login account by anyone. At this stage, all other detected changes can be reconciled to authorized requests for change. We need to immediately declare an information security incident and begin by disabling the SysBackup123 account."*

What We Have Built And What We Are Likely To Hear

We have gained insight into management intentions and the direction of the business, so we can focus on what matters most. We are aware of previous IT control issues that may still be problematic. Through our situational awareness, we know which areas of the business will be easier to tackle and which will require more attention.

We have integrated information security into change management, which has significantly enhanced our situational awareness and enables us to influence future changes. By improving change management, we advance the objectives of IT operations, information security, and IT overall, and we reduce friendly fire. We've started to build a trusted relationship with change management so that we can comfortably walk up to the change manager and say, "Hey, can you give me a list of change requests for those services that have specific information security risks, and show me the change schedule for those assets? I want to make sure we're managing those risks because we have a quarterly audit next week."

By reducing the number of people with access privileges, we've reduced the opportunity for errors, catastrophic failures, and information security breaches. Account revocation is now part of employee transfer and termination processes. This has reduced the number of ghost accounts, resulting in lower risk to the organization (and fewer easy targets for auditors to find). As a result, IT spends less time preparing for audits and ultimately there are fewer findings.

We have defined roles, responsibilities, and escalation procedures, thereby reducing needless interruptions between IT operations and information security. Incident management knows when to engage information security. We're also collecting meaningful forensics on what changed to help in our information security investigations. Incident management has a relevant timeline of authorized, scheduled, and detected changes, so we can meaningfully explain what changed. Consequently, we improve first fix rates, decrease MTTR and reduce the number of inappropriate escalations.

> *"When we completed the steps documented in this first phase, we learned what kind of shape we're in, including the good, the bad, and the really ugly. Without having this awareness, we would be doomed to keep making the same mistakes over and over again. Our goal is to break the cycle of merely surviving between failures. By gaining awareness and building effective controls, we started to confidently know where we needed to focus our efforts in the next phases. While adding or updating controls may cause some initial problems, they are offset by the many gains in stability and security."*—PETER PERFETTI, DIRECTOR, IT SECURITY AND RISK MANAGEMENT

> *"Information security organizations that follow the approach in this phase will find IT operations much easier to work, because information security will be using the existing IT operational processes to achieve security goals. By doing this, information security will be working with, as opposed to against, IT operations. Security becomes just another part of the daily workflow and templates, which IT operations staff thrives on. This makes security training and compliance become much easier. Information security is better armed when they get involved and can react faster knowing that specific procedures have been followed and desired information obtained by IT operations."*—STEVE DARBY, VP OF OPERATIONS, IP SERVICES

Phase 2: Find Business Risks And Fix Fragile Artifacts

What Are We Going To Do?

In the previous phase, we established situational awareness and inserted information security controls into IT operations. However, the problem remains that the information security risks to the organization are potentially limitless, but information security has finite time and resources to address them. Where should we focus?

This is the problem we address in Phase 2. In this phase, we identify where the highest business risks are, discover where the business is relying most upon critical IT functionality, and take steps to ensure that adequate controls exist and are effective.

In this phase, we create a focusing mechanism by taking a top-down, risk-based approach to understand where the business has placed reliance on critical IT functionality (we fully define these terms later), and then identify what information security controls are needed to protect critical functionality and data. We then find and fix any information security control gaps, in order of priority.

As information security practitioners, we may have been exposed to top-down, risk-based approaches in support of audits. However, as information security practitioners, we need to take the lead in defining and protecting what matters. We cannot wait until the next audit cycle to find out if we're doing things correctly, because then it's already too late! We may have missed a critical area of risk that went completely unaddressed, or, just as bad, we may have spent valuable time and resources securing IT services and systems that did not really matter.

We will leave this phase with confidence that we are focusing on the right things, have controls integrated into daily operations, and can leverage those controls so we can quickly detect and correct information security incidents. We will also have evidence that controls are working when the auditors show up, and be able to map all IT services to regulatory requirements and required supporting control objectives across the enterprise.

Issues And Indicators

Visible Ops Security Phase 2 tackles the following issues:

Issues	Narrative Example
Information security often can't focus its efforts on the top risk areas	We have hundreds of business applications that we need to secure and support. They run on thousands of servers and hundreds of databases, all connected together by countless network switches, which are partitioned by at least two hundred firewalls.
	There is just no way that our information security team can stay on top of it all. We are spread way too thin. I figure that each one of us is covering hundreds of systems and thousands of controls. How do we really know where to focus our efforts? If we don't focus, we won't get anything done. And we won't really find and fix the important risks that matter.
	But, of all the thousands and thousands of systems, where should we focus first?
Organizations are buried by regulatory compliance and audit requirements	Every industry that our organization operates in has more and more compliance requirements that IT is responsible for. In fact, it seems like every new office we open in a different geography brings us an additional set of regulatory requirements. On top of that, now every customer and supplier wants us to accredit that our systems are secure, and are sending their auditors to inspect us!
	We are now buried in paperwork and filling out forms for auditors. It doesn't help that we take a compliance-du-jour approach to everything. As soon as we took care of SOX-404, we got hit by PCI. When we got done with PCI, we got buried with HIPAA-related work.
	We're no longer an information security shop. We're paper pushers.
Must repeat audit work year after year	We are repeating a lot of documentation and substantiation work for IT controls, especially because we handle each regulation separately. Last year we spent thousands of hours on this. And we're going to do it all over again this year.
	Why? Because instead of building controls into daily IT operations, we substantiate the presence of controls after the fact. We spend days trying to generate a report that will convince the auditors to believe that there were no unauthorized changes and no unauthorized access!
	I'll admit that I learned a lot in the first couple of years of this, but this is turning into pure tedium, and is taking us away from other very important projects. Plus we're finding that we're having to paper over some real information security issues that should never have happened in the first place if we were doing things right.
	Looking at this game of charades that we're playing, I wonder at times whether we could have just done the right thing. Instead of pretending we have controls, maybe it would have been cheaper to just implement the controls. I think the auditors are starting to catch on that we don't actually have meaningful controls, because they're beginning to ask tougher questions.
Bottom-up IT controls scoping leads to lots of urgent but ultimately, irrelevant, and unnecessary work	We worked heroically on SOX-404 audit prep work, mobilizing more than 50 people to meet the compliance deadlines. The auditors still identified a long list of deficiencies, and in countless meetings with the financial auditors and business management, we managed to argue that none of the deficiencies would result in an undetected material financial reporting error.
	On the one hand, everyone was relieved that we dodged a bullet.
	However, two things really started to bother me. First, if none of that audit prep work was necessary, why did we do all that work and waste all that time? Second, there are real information security risks that we could have corrected had we acted on the audit findings.
	There's got to be a better way!

Issues	Narrative Example
Following letter of the law, not spirit of the law	There's such a big rush to comply with the letter of the law, but there's no real interest in following the spirit and intent of the law. Management gives us just enough resources to show compliance, but never enough to actually close the information security holes.
	Because we're not actually fixing things, we know we'll be doing this same exercise a year from now when the auditors come back.
Top-down risk-based processes never finish	There's some hope that the new Enterprise Risk Management (ERM) task force will address some of these issues. That team includes some of the most senior managers in the company, and they are definitely taking a top-down, risk-based approach.
	The problem is that they've been at it for three years, and there are no indications that the consultants they're using are ever going to leave. In fact, the only certain thing is their next invoice, and another one of their horrible half-day workshops.
	This is almost as bad as the "six month ITIL configuration management database (CMDB) project," which still hasn't been completed two years later. They start at the top level, prototype it, and debug it, but I've never seen one completed and adding real value to the business on a sustaining and regular basis. It just never really impacts daily operations.

How Are We Going To Do It?

In the original *Visible Ops Handbook*, Phase 2 describes the following steps: Catch and Release, and Fix Fragile Artifacts. The purpose of these steps was to start understanding which IT services were the most fragile—that is, the IT services and systems that had the highest business outage or impairment costs, lowest change success rates, and longest mean time to repair.

The goal was to start understanding and documenting the relationships between IT services and assets (i.e., configuration items or CIs), so we can replace those fragile artifacts with stable and secure builds. And, by making those repeatable builds "cheaper to rebuild than to repair" in Phase 3, we would dramatically reduce repair times by treating production systems like fuses (i.e., we will no longer repair fuses, but replace them with identical fuses, quickly and predictably).

In *Visible Ops Security*, we extend the focus of Phase 2 beyond just operational risks, to those risks relevant to information security, compliance, and financial reporting. To make sure that we focus on what really matters, we go through an explicit scoping step for IT services and systems to ensure that we can always explicitly link information security controls to risks that can affect the achievement of business objectives or requirements.

Note that we are not focusing just on mitigating IT risks that could jeopardize financial reporting objectives, such as those in support of SOX-404. Instead, we are ensuring that the right information security controls are in place so the organization can achieve all of its goals.

In this phase, we will do the following:

- Establish an initial scope of the business processes and IT services and systems that really matter by using a top-down, risk-based approach.

- Cover the periphery—Because of the significant political consequences of an information security incident involving externally facing systems, we create a list of these IT services and systems as candidates to investigate further. These are the systems that we cannot afford to have an information security-related incident on because of the risk of front-page news, brand damage, regulatory fines, etc.

- Zoom out to rule out—Our goal in this step is to confirm that there is actually reliance (defined in the next section) on critical IT functionality, so that we can ensure that IT controls actually protect a business objective or risk. The goal is to continue a top-down, risk-based approach. Specifically, we want to ensure that we are not making the mistake of taking a bottom-up approach. We will constantly remind ourselves that there is no such thing as technology risk, only business risk caused by technology.

- Find and fix IT controls issues—Now that we have confirmed where there is reliance on IT functionality, we must determine if the existing IT controls sufficiently mitigate those business risks. We must compensate or correct those areas where IT controls are insufficient, notify the appropriate stakeholders, and help get them fixed.

- Streamline IT controls for regulatory compliance—After we gain assurance in the IT controls that support critical IT functionality, we create a common approach to IT controls so that they can be reused in as many audit and compliance programs as possible. Our goal is to eliminate the "compliance-du-jour" problem. Instead, we will have a single "high water mark" that we can use for all the relevant IT compliance requirements, and that IT operations and information security can manage to.

Defining "Top-Down, Risk-Based Approach" And "Reliance"

To enable appropriate scoping, which can result in a dramatic reduction in the scope of information security IT controls, we will be using extensively the three concepts of *top-down, risk-based approach*, *reliance*, and *critical IT functionality*.

A top-down, risk-based approach allows us to use business risk to focus on what matters. The PCAOB[20] published the following definition of the top-down, risk-based approach to motivate the continuing need to focus on the financial reporting and business risks that matter, instead of auditing everything:

> "In a top-down approach …, the auditor performs procedures to obtain the necessary understanding of internal control over financial reporting and to identify the controls to test in a sequential manner, starting with company-level controls and then driving down to significant accounts, significant processes, and, finally, individual controls at the process, transaction, or application levels. Auditing Standard No. 2 [and its successor, Auditing Standard No. 5] was designed to encourage the auditor to take this type of top-down approach to his or her audit."[21]

Contrast this to a bottom-up approach, which focuses first on technology risks and threats. For example, we enter our IP network address range into the vulnerability scanning tool, let it scan the network, and then we panic when we see the 2,000 pages

---

[20] Public Company Accounting Oversight Board (PCAOB) is responsible for oversight of the CPA firms that audit the financial statements of companies publicly listed on the SEC. http://www.pcaobus.org
[21] PCAOB Staff Q&A #38

of vulnerabilities. We then try to prioritize our corrective actions based on what the tool recommends, which sorts the findings by the technology vulnerabilities that are easiest to exploit. The problem is that we will take corrective actions without understanding whether a significant business risk could result from the vulnerability (e.g., perhaps ignoring important information, such as the fact that all of the servers are actually decommissioned and no longer in use).

Although the PCAOB discussion of the top-down, risk-based approach is very focused on internal controls for financial reporting, it is equally applicable for other internal control objectives, such as for information security, compliance with laws and regulations, and operations. Using this approach is even possible for technology-specific compliance requirements, such as PCI DSS (Payment Card Industry Data Security Standard). We could even argue that using a top-down, risk-based approach is even more critical, as a bottom-up approach will fail due to the inability to focus, causing us to bleed to death before we can apply the nearly infinite number of bandages it requires.

To put the top-down, risk-based philosophy into practice, we need to introduce the concept of *reliance*. An organization has placed *reliance* on a control when the achievement of a business process goal hinges on the design and operating effectiveness of that control. In other words, if that control fails, an undetected error may prevent the business objective from being met (e.g., processing customer orders, issuing accurate financial statements, securing confidential customer and PII data, and passing the PCI compliance requirements.)

Reliance is placed on an IT control when the control provides *critical functionality* that must operate as designed in order to detect or prevent errors. Critical functionality is the logic in a system that enables attainment of objectives. For financial reporting, it is often calculations or a control necessary to ensure the integrity of account balances and outputs. For IT operations, it is often the functionality of all of the components of the IT service required to fulfill the business objectives, of which any impairment will negatively impact the business.

Here are several examples of when there is reliance on an IT control:

- For SOX-404 financial reporting for the accounts payable process, suppose that reliance is placed on an automated three-way match control in the ERP system that ensures that only invoices with valid purchase orders and packing slips are paid. As long as the three-way match setting is enabled and does not change, we can trust the results of the accounts payable process that is enabled by the ERP system.

  Consequently, IT management must prove that no unauthorized changes were made to that three-way match setting. Why? Because an unauthorized change could disarm the IT functionality that we rely upon, which could result in an undetected financial statement error. (e.g., we rely on the correct configuration of the three-way match setting, which then relies on effective change controls.)

- For daily operations of the Web auction ordering business process, reliance is placed on all the IT services and systems that deliver critical functionality that must be available to process customer orders. This critical functionality includes the Web site that delivers the user presentation, the Java code that creates the Web presentation, the databases, operating systems, and networking devices, as well as the interfaces to the business systems where customer transactions are uploaded.

To safeguard the objective of high availability and ability to process revenue, change management controls are necessary to ensure that all changes to the various components are properly reviewed and authorized, and that no untested or unauthorized changes are implemented. Why? Because an uncontrolled change could disrupt company operations. (i.e., we rely on the proper functioning of all order entry IT services for operations, which then relies on effective change controls.)

- For compliance with emissions laws and regulations in a petroleum company, reliance may be placed on sensors in the smokestacks of refining plants. These sensors are used to support the assertion that the refinery's emissions are in compliance with laws and regulations. These sensors are monitored by IT services, and reliance is placed on the correct functioning of the sensors, as well as on the supporting IT services.

To safeguard the objective of complying with emissions laws, we need to control changes that could impair the critical functionality of these sensor services. Uncontrolled change could result in management's inability to validate actual outputs and potentially result in fines and lawsuits.

What can go wrong? Often, IT and information security erroneously assume that there is reliance on an IT service, system, or control within a given business process. In many cases, reliance is actually placed on a control downstream in the business process, not in the IT service.

Another common mistake that could be averted by better understanding reliance is when information security believes that there is a significant technology vulnerability that must be mitigated to safeguard a given IT service, when in fact there are adequate business controls that would detect and correct any failure. When erroneous assumptions of reliance are made and acted upon, significant amounts of valuable time and resources can be spent on the implementation and ongoing maintenance of unnecessary IT controls.[22]

A SOX-404 Cautionary Tale

When external auditors started testing against SOX-404 in the first year, IT findings represented the largest category of findings, totaling more than the combined findings in the revenue, procure-to-pay, and tax categories.[23] It's estimated that as much as $3 billion was spent in the first year of SOX-404 to fix IT controls to remediate these findings. Ultimately, most of these findings were found not to be direct risks to accurate financial reports and did not result in a material weakness. This is because they followed a bottom up versus a top-down, risk-based approach.

---

[22] In the 2006 IT Controls Performance Study and the repeat ITPI study funded by the Institute of Internal Auditors, there was always a group of IT organizations that had more controls, but were not getting the performance benefits of the control. The conjecture was the IT management was grudgingly implementing controls purely to satisfy audit, as opposed to getting daily operational value. The authors describe this group of IT organizations as those that are "smoking more and enjoying it less."

[23] KPMG study: "Sarbanes-Oxley 404: Lessons Learned", ISACA Luncheon Sessions, April 20, 2005.

Consider the following scenario: The SOX-404 team asks for an information security review of a WebSphere server that runs the materials management systems. The review shows that it's a custom WebSphere application running on a cluster of servers that is connected to a clustered Oracle database. We then locate the firewall and determine the segment it's on.

An information security review of the materials management system uncovers:

- Numerous ghost accounts.
- A lack of password aging policies.
- Critical vulnerabilities in the Java code, including cross-site scripting issues in the HTML.
- Vulnerabilities in the Oracle database configuration.
- Firewall rules that are suspect and need further investigation.

Our task list keeps expanding and the internal auditors are showing up next week. We decide to focus on the operating system level, and our suspicions prove to be correct: The operating system is not running at the latest patch levels. We add this to our list of corrective actions that need to be taken right away, and start talking with the owners of the operating system, database, and application, and even the firewall team.

When the internal audit team comes in, we are candid and transparent about all the issues. Management is informed about the risks, and soon 50+ people are working on all these issues, dropping other high-priority projects to get these issues fixed in time. After all, the argument is made, these issues should be fixed eventually because they do represent risk.

But there just isn't enough time. The external auditors come in and find all of these issues. They start preparing a management letter stating that the integrity of the IT general control process (ITGC) environment cannot be substantiated.

As a result, more high-level meetings take place, and the financial people start to argue that the ITGC issues really can't lead to an undetected financial reporting error. They pull out the "nine firm document" and use something called "Chart Three" to make the case.[24] Then management and the CPA firms argue back and forth about the linkage, and management starts bringing in all the business experts to show that a failure in the ITGCs for this system could not result in inaccurate financial reports.

Finally, the owner of the materials management business process determines that even if the application, database, operating system, and firewall were compromised by a person trying to perpetrate fraud, the attempt would be caught by a daily financial reconciliation between the materials management inventory report and another report from the ERP system.

Given this new evidence, everyone agrees that reliance is actually placed on the daily financial reconciliation, which would catch both fraud and errors. Furthermore, they agree that reliance is not placed on the IT system and the supporting ITGCs. So, the IT systems are out of scope, and no further IT testing is required.

---

[24] Evaluating IT Control Deficiencies. http://www.theiia.org/ITAudit/index.cfm?act=itaudit.archive&fid=5581

Everyone is relieved. As the information security practitioners, however, we struggle with this unsettling question about why we went through all this trouble if our efforts were not required to substantiate the accuracy of financial statements. Furthermore, we wonder if all the "good hygiene habits" are actually important and can be justified.

To be clear, it's not that the downstream manual financial reconciliation control is the best control possible. The point is that if the scoping of IT controls were done correctly in the first place, the only control weaknesses that we would have tested and found would be those that truly jeopardized accurate financial reporting. Instead, we found control weaknesses on systems that were out of scope, and then kept digging needlessly.

Dangers Of "Bottom-up" Auditing

The cautionary tale resulted from a bottom-up approach, which acted upon perceived vulnerabilities and threats without first identifying actual business risks, which cannot be derived at the technology level alone. The danger of such an approach is that many control deficiencies may be discovered that do not actually reflect business risk and do not require action. If we don't realize this, we'll waste valuable resources on correcting these deficiencies. This is most evident when we are dealing with financial reporting internal control objectives, but it is equally applicable for information security, compliance, and operations.

Much of the throw-away work done during the first year of SOX compliance is a result of a bottom-up approach. The resulting IT testing efforts consumed a colossal amount of effort and money. Close scrutiny showed that many issues did not actually jeopardize financial reporting goals. As a result, in 2005, the PCAOB notified external auditors that a top-down approach was required.[25]

At the same time, organizations began moving to a risk-based approach in an attempt to reduce the costs of unnecessary controls. Despite the shift in audit's approach, the reality is that top-down, risk-based approaches are still rare.

The Gait[26] Principles And Methodology

To apply the top-down, risk-based approach, we use the GAIT[27] principles and methodology, developed by the Institute of Internal Auditors. GAIT is a set of four principles and a methodology that can be used to scope IT general control processes that need to be included in the assessment of internal controls over financial reporting. The GAIT-R principles expand GAIT to allow its use for analyzing how IT affects the achievement of all business goals and objectives.

The GAIT-R principles are:[28]

- **Principle 1**—The failure of technology is only a risk that needs to be assessed, managed, and audited if it represents a risk to the business.

[25] PCAOB Release 2005-023. November 30, 2005. http://www.pcaobus.com/rules/docket_014/2005-11-30_release_2005-023.pdf

[26] Copyright 2008, GAIT by The Institute of Internal Auditors Research Foundation, 247 Maitland Avenue, Altamonte Springs, Florida 32701-4201 U.S.A. Reprinted with permission.

[27] GAIT stands for Guide to the Assessment of IT General Controls Scope Based on Risk (GAIT)

[28] "The GAIT Principles," The Institute of Internal Auditors, January 2007 (http://www.theiia.org/guidance/technology/gait/)

- **Principle 2**—Key controls should be identified as the result of a top-down assessment of business risk, risk tolerance, and the controls (including automated controls and IT general controls) required to manage or mitigate business risk.

- **Principle 3**—Business risks are mitigated by a combination of manual and automated key controls. To assess the system of internal control to manage/mitigate business risks, key automated controls need to be assessed.

- **Principle 4**—IT general controls may be relied upon to provide assurance of the continued and proper operation of automated key controls (e.g., change management, access information security, and operations[29]).

  — **Principle 4a**—The IT general control process risks that need to be identified are those that affect critical IT functionality in significant applications and related data.

  — **Principle 4b**—The IT general control process risks that need to be identified exist in processes and at various IT layers: application program code, databases, operating systems, and network.

  — **Principle 4c**—Risks in IT general control processes are mitigated by the achievement of IT control objectives, not individual controls.

The steps we will take are adapted from the GAIT methodology.[30]

Again, our goal is not to become auditors. However, internal auditors cannot be the only people who can determine what is important enough to warrant attention for IT controls. Otherwise, information security and IT operations will always be at risk of working on the wrong things until the next audit cycle. Ideally, all three groups agree on what the top risks are to the organization, so IT operations and information security can collaborate to mitigate those risks and help the organization achieve its goals, and audit can provide independent assurance by confirming that IT controls are effective. So, we will use the best tools we can find to create this common view of organizational objectives, risks, and controls.

Step 1: Establish Our Business Process Worry List

In Phase 1, we increased our situational awareness. We learned what senior management and the business are trying to achieve, and what they want from information security. We know how these business units are organized and what they worry about, the IT services that support them, and IT processes that support the IT services. We also identified high-level risk indicators from the past to help us understand if there are IT control issues.

Our goal is to take all this information and to create a prioritized list of IT services, ranked in order of importance to the business, to understand what control requirements they have (e.g., in support of financial reporting, compliance, and/or operations). In this step, we will take the situational awareness that we generated in Phase 1 and turn it into our business process worry list. We will consider adding any externally facing IT systems, and then confirm this list with the business.

---

[29] GAIT defines *operations* as the responsibility to deliver IT services and the ability to restore service when interrupted at inopportune times. This would include the ITIL processes of incident and problem management, service continuity and disaster recovery, service design, and so forth.

[30] The GAIT Methodology can be found with the GAIT materials, as well as scenarios and examples of its applications.

Task 1: Cover the periphery by considering externally facing systems

In addition to the business process worry list derived from the situational awareness that we built in Phase 1, we must also consider whether any externally facing IT infrastructure needs to be added to our list. Why? The visibility, perceived criticality, and political ramifications of an information security incident from externally facing IT systems being compromised are often extremely high.

By focusing on the network periphery, even though it may appear that we are taking a bottom-up approach, we aren't. We can still get in very deep trouble if someone hacks a low-priority FTP server, resulting in front page news. For example, senior management may care that this FTP server is hacked and then used to distribute confidential information or PII. In certain industries, such as healthcare, this could result in brand and reputation damage, loss of customers, fines, class action lawsuits, or even the risk of new laws being enacted in an attempt to protect patients. These are serious risks that we need to mitigate!

So, in this task, we make sure we have adequate situational awareness of externally facing IT systems, so that we are aware of what the externally facing systems are, we know their purpose, any regulatory requirements, political climate, presence of confidential data, and we understand the potential risks to the business.

To accomplish this, we:

- Document externally facing IT systems.
- Understand their business purpose, including:
  - Public and customer facing applications
  - Network-to-network VPN connections
  - Vendor or partner site on Internet (such as a portal or ftp site)
  - Vendor or partner site on secured connection (such as a VPN or leased line)
  - Outsourced services (e.g., logistics, development, HR, or payroll)
- Identify their business and IT owners.

Task 2: Discover and understand externally facing IT systems

An externally facing IT system is any system that is visible in some manner to people outside the business—partners, suppliers, customers, and so forth. In the most literal interpretation, externally facing systems are those systems that are visible from outside the organization (e.g., public IP addresses).

Externally facing is by no means limited to *Internet facing*. Frame-relay, point-to-point T1 connections with partners, value-added networks, and wireless networks accessible in the parking lot are other examples of systems that are also visible to the outside world.

Our goal is to assemble the list of externally facing systems, understand what they are being used for, map them back to a business process, and understand what the business risks are. Then we will add that business process to our business process worry list.

Many IT organizations can quickly come up with a list of the obvious front-end systems—the primary Web servers, file transfer servers (e.g., FTP servers), VPN servers, e-mail, etc. Unfortunately, hundreds of services that are just as important (or maybe even more important) are probably missing from the list, including the data interfaces or business service interfaces that glue the business processes, various systems, and even multiple organizations together. Here are a few examples to illustrate the point:

- **Enterprise application integration (EAI) tools**—Organizations running disparate ERP systems may exchange data through EAI tools (e.g., BizTalk, Tibco, and SAP interfaces), which translates between the disparate systems. The risk is that EAI tools reside on operating systems, Web servers, or FTP servers that may not be adequately patched or protected. The risk is that confidentiality, integrity, or availability may be compromised, resulting in IP leakage and disruption of operations.

- **File transfer servers**—Supply chain partners often have a file transfer server where numerous partners may upload sensitive transactions into a single directory. Vendors may have read/write access to the server. Or, all vendors may log in anonymously, or with user IDs and passwords that never change. The risk is that intellectual property or confidential data may be leaked. The competitive and legal ramifications could be serious.

- **Vendor portals**—Companies often have HR portals that link to one or more insurance portals to consolidate insurance plans. The portal makes information accessible by employees and their families from home. This portal service runs on a Web server that stores personally identifiable information. It may lack adequate password controls for privileged users. It may exchange sensitive data as plain text to partner portals, or store the data in a manner that is not properly protected. The risk is noncompliance with legal mandates such as the Health Insurance Portability and Accountability Act and state data privacy statutes.

As information security professionals, we should be paranoid and assume we don't know everything. After all, we've been burned in the past by things we didn't know about. Being appropriately paranoid, we scan the list of public IP addresses (local, remote, and at co-location facilities) to make sure that we know about each system that responds to a ping sweep or port scan. We then reconcile the list of detected systems against our known list of externally facing systems.

For all unknown IP addresses, we have to determine if the address belongs to a critical host by reconciling the asset to critical business processes. If the system is part of a critical business process, we add it to the list of services to be investigated and verify that the IT resources that support these services are covered by the change management processes implemented in Phase 1.

We now have a more complete business process worry list, which includes the critical business systems that are externally facing. The next thing we need to do is verify the business process worry list with the business, to make sure the processes on the list are actually worth worrying about.

Task 3: Verify Our Business Process Worry List

When we generated our initial situational awareness during Phase 1, we worked with the business to prioritize all the IT services. What we are missing now is validation. So, we need to take our business process worry list and verify our list with one or more groups who already have a global business view. The good news is that many groups may already have this perspective, including:

- Internal audit
- Business continuity
- Finance and accounting
- Strategic planning
- Compliance office
- Enterprise risk management

In general, our phone call with each of the groups can be started off similarly:

> *"I bet you're tired of information security failing to protect what matters, a compliance-du-jour approach, and information security wasting time and resources on technology risks that are largely irrelevant. I sure am tired of these issues. So, to address this, we've created a list of prioritized IT services that we need to protect, because we can't do everything. We've also tried to understand any compliance and control requirements for each of these that information security can assist with.*
>
> *"Can you help us review the list and make sure that we have the proper perspective and understand whether any critical IT functionality is in that process and where reliance is placed? This way, we can start scoping the work, and then find and fix any IT control issues"*

Out of these meetings, we will have gained confidence in our prioritized list of IT services and any associated compliance and control requirements.

Step 2: Work The List, Zoom Out To Rule Out

In this step, we systematically look at each of the business processes (and externally facing systems) on our business process worry list. Our purpose is to understand whether there is *reliance* or *critical functionality* on any IT systems for each business process.

To make sure we don't mistakenly assume reliance (as we did in the SOX-404 Cautionary Tale), we must understand where reliance is really placed in each business process. To do this, we must zoom out to understand the end-to-end business transaction and activity flow, getting as much help as we can from business management, analysts, and auditors. (Audit will often have flowcharts and narratives for each business process in detail. Generating this was a lot of work, so if we can get this from audit, we are in luck!) Having this high-level view helps us figure out the extent to which the IT risks in the business process actually jeopardize business goals.

Only after we confirm that there is reliance and critical IT functionality can we go to the next step, which is to zoom back in to understand how the functionality is delivered, where the data resides, and where the real business risks are. This understanding enables us to identify which IT controls are necessary to protect critical IT functionality.

Task 1: Get help to zoom out to rule out

We will use GAIT-R Principle 4a to confirm that the business process on our worry list is significant enough to warrant our attention. We must confirm with the business that reliance is placed on critical IT functionality that we must safeguard.

To do this correctly, we definitely need help from someone who understands the end-to-end business processes and controls, such as a business analyst or auditor. So, we must pick up the phone and call this person. We will start the conversation with the following:

> *"I bet you're tired of not being able to determine the appropriate scope for IT controls in support of internal control objectives. I bet you're frustrated that it's often difficult to communicate effectively with IT audit and information security.*

> *"Maybe you feel like business auditors throw things over the wall to IT audit and information security, and in return, we throw findings back over the wall at you. And the findings may not represent a real risk to the business objectives.*

> *"I'd like to see if we can fix this by making sure we create an integrated understanding of the business processes on the worry list that I've collected from the business. I would like your help to confirm whether these business processes are significant enough to worry about, identify the critical IT functionality and automated controls, and substantiate that we really have placed reliance there. If you can help me do that, I can work to ensure that we have IT controls that can safeguard that critical IT functionality.*

> *"Can we meet to discuss this further and document our thinking on critical IT functionality, reliance, and linking this to IT controls?"*

The reason we need considerable help from someone like a business auditor or analyst is that we need to get the following information for each of the business processes on our worry list. The questions are listed below, and then explanations provided in the following tasks.

- Is the business process sufficiently significant in context of the goal? (e.g., maximizing profits and saving lives.)

- For financial reporting goals, we also ask whether the business process is sufficiently complex? (Because complexity tends to increase reliance on critical IT functionality.)

- What are all the fully automated IT controls? (e.g., application controls such as matching or updating accounts in the general ledger and automated sensors for emissions compliance.)

- What are the key manual controls that rely on application functionality? (e.g., reconciliations that use reports generated by IT systems.)

Task 2: Get confirmation of business process significance and complexity

For each business process, we must first confirm:

- That the business process materially affects a significant account (for financial reporting) or that the achievement of the business process objectives represents a significant portion of the organizational goals.
- That the business process is sufficiently complex. Complex business processes have higher reliance on critical IT functionality, not only to achieve objectives, but also to state that the process is operating as designed, as well as for the mitigation of risk.

Highly complex business processes typically have such a high degree of automation and/or volume of transactions that without IT, we cannot achieve the objectives or reconstruct the results manually. In other words, if the IT systems malfunctioned, we would not know, or we would have a very difficult time correcting and/or recovering from the failure.

An interesting example occurred in April 2007, when the Alaska Department of Revenue disclosed that an employee accidentally deleted not only the data for application forms to receive dividends worth $38 billion but also the backup drive. Worse, the backup tapes were unreadable. The organization had to re-enter nine months of data from 300 boxes of papers, requiring more than 70 people to work overtime, including weekends, for two months. The cost exceeded $220,000.[31]

Consequently, for highly complex business processes, the controls need to be inside the IT system, as opposed to outside the IT system. Consider the following examples:

- Significant and complex business processes (that has critical IT functionality):
  — Online auction payment settlement that does millions of auction transactions per day.
  — Program trading of derivative financial instruments for a $20 billion mutual fund.
- Significant and noncomplex automated processes (that does not have critical IT functionality):
  — Payroll processes for salaried employees in an organization of 10 employees, where salaries change once per year and there is no turnover. (Salary changes can be manually inspected.)
  — Grain inventory levels that are centrally located. (Grain inventory can be manually confirmed by visually inspecting the grain level in each silo.)

With the business analyst or auditor, we can now answer the question "Is the business process significant and complex?" For financial reporting internal control objectives, if it is not both significant and complex, we can often scope this business process out, along with all the associated IT controls. This is because we can manually and substantively confirm account balances and values by examining the inputs and outputs of the IT system. (e.g., we can count that we have 20 beans before it went into the IT system, and we can count 20 beans afterwards, so we can conclude that no beans were lost.)

---

[31] http://www.computerworld.com/action/article.do?command=viewArticleBasic&articleId=9013968

Task 3: Get documentation on where reliance on critical IT functionality is placed in the business process

For business processes that are in scope, we must now document the critical IT functionality that is relied upon to prevent and detect errors. Again, we work with the business analysts or auditors because they are already most likely familiar with the business process as a result of their top-down, risk-based audit. Ideally, we would get copies of their work papers, including narratives, flow charts, and other documentation of critical systems and application controls that they have documented.[32] Although we want audit to remain independent and objective, it is possible to leverage their efforts and expertise around the business process risks and application controls.

Ideally, the business analyst or auditor can answer the following questions, which will precisely identify the critical IT functionality we need to protect through correctly designed and operating IT controls:

- What are all the fully automated IT controls? (e.g., application controls such as matching or updating accounts in the general ledger and automated sensors for emissions compliance.)

- What are the key manual controls that rely on application functionality? (e.g., reconciliations that use reports generated by IT systems.)

- Is there other critical application functionality?

Consider the following examples:

- A 911 application helps the police department of a large metropolitan city fulfill its mission to protect and serve the citizens of the city. The application handles many emergency calls per minute, dispatching alerts to hundreds of other locations and organizations (e.g., fire departments, hospitals, and ambulances).

This is significant and complex. The critical functionality is to create incident records from emergency calls to mobilize emergency services, including SWAT teams. In this scenario, there are no downstream compensating controls to detect unauthorized access. Consequently, false records inserted into the application could result in a SWAT team being dispatched, breaking down the door of an innocent family with drawn firearms at the ready, creating the risk of loss of life.[33] Therefore, the business process relies not only on critical IT functionality but also on IT general control processes to protect critical functionality and, furthermore, ensure that all incident records are authorized.

- A business uses its materials management application to manage risks by limiting receipts to not more than 10 percent over the quantity specified on a purchase order. Why? Suppose the purchasing department orders 40,000 pounds of paper. The first business risk is that an unscrupulous vendor will send more than was ordered to inflate the sale. The second risk is that an employee in receiving accidentally adds a zero, and due to the error, we pay the vendor for ten times the actual amount. The data entry error has additional consequences. The people scheduling and running the printing presses believe we have 10 times more paper than we have. Moreover,

---

[32] Narratives are written descriptions of the process that are often used by auditors when existing process documentation is not present. Work papers are the documentation collected by an audit team during an audit engagement.

[33] This actually happened in Orange County, California on March 29, 2007. http://www.ocregister.com/news/home-emami-county-1894171-ellis-system

the value of raw materials is overstated because the fictitious paper is carried on the books at standard cost.

To mitigate these risks IT implements reasonableness checks on data entry input for the screens used by receiving personnel. In addition, accounts payable requires a three-way match before payment is made.[34] Finally, weekly variance reports analyze differences in quantities ordered, received, and invoiced to verify that the processes and system are working as expected.

- Suppose we have an IT application that performs a rebate approval process that does all nonstandard pricing approvals and that 20 percent of all sales go through, thus making it significant. The application is also complex. It has critical IT functionality present because changes to calculations could result in financial reporting errors and inappropriate authorizations.

  Key automated controls include restricting approval of nonstandard prices to authorized managers and routing of nonstandard prices to authorized managers for approval.

We understand what the business risks are and the critical IT functionality (including application controls) that are responsible for mitigating these risks. Now, we need to verify that the controls responsible for protecting critical IT functionality are in place.

Task 4: Zoom in for a better view

We have firmly established that the business process is in scope, and that there is critical IT functionality, which brings the IT general control processes into scope. We have been working with the business analyst or auditor up to this point, but now we have all the information that we need to take it from here. Our task now is to understand what could go wrong at the IT technology layers (i.e., application, database, operating system, and network) that could jeopardize critical IT functionality and the integrity of the data, and ensure that sufficient controls exist to mitigate those risks.

To do this, we will do the following for each of the business processes in scope:

- For each IT service, we record:
    - The business process being supported.
    - Relevant internal control objectives (e.g., financial reporting, information security, compliance, operations).
    - Any applicable regulations.
    - Where critical data is stored that cannot be compromised (e.g., confidential information, PII, and financial records).
- We create a list of all configuration items (CIs) that support the IT service, categorizing them into one of the following technology layers: application, database, operating system, or network.

---

[34] The three-way match function enforces a control that requires the following before accounts payable issues a check to a vendor: a valid purchase order, a confirmed receipt into inventory by receiving personnel, and a valid invoice from the vendor.

- For each CI, we record the following (at a minimum):
  — IP address and host name
  — Parent/child relationships

We also include from our situational awareness work in Phase 1 any high level risk indicators (e.g., any repeat audit findings, lawsuits, recurring outages, or service level issues). We must next move beyond inventory data and understand more about what the service does and why. To do this, let's review the following example:

> The rebate approval process application is used for processing nonstandard customer pricing. The application was developed in house, written in J2EE, and has been in operations for more than four years. The application follows a quarterly release cycle wherein all non-emergency updates and patches are applied. Approximately 1,000 people use this application on a regular basis.

> The application runs on Microsoft SQL Server. The application, databases, and operating systems are patched quarterly. During analysis, two major risks are identified: The DBAs have access to the production database and could inject information that bypasses the application. During an information security review, it was identified that a significant amount of application functionality actually resides in database stored procedures that the DBAs can modify at will. The client application handles user input that transits the network and a network incident that hampers traffic could result in loss of data.

> In regards to this application, there is a risk that rebate-related accounts (both income statement and balance sheet) may be materially misstated due to unauthorized rebates, incorrectly calculated rebates and/or incomplete accounting for rebates due.

Next, we must review each layer of the technology stack[35] to understand what could go wrong. For each layer we ask what the relevant IT general control processes are, what risks they are intended to mitigate, control objectives for the layer and whether the control is in scope. Appendix A shows a sample analysis.

The following demonstrates the thought process we go through to populate the table in Appendix A showing how we ask "what can go wrong at each IT layer of the stack that could jeopardize critical IT functionality":

- At the application layer, there is a risk that an unauthorized, untested, or otherwise problematic application change could result in an undetected error in the financial statements. Consequently, we need to substantiate that there are change management controls that mitigate these risks, and ensure that accruals are complete and accurately calculated. We conclude that change management at the application layer is in scope.

- At the database layer, there is a risk that data is not being appropriately backed up or that we cannot restore data, which would prevent lost and corrupt pricing data from being recovered. Therefore, we conclude that data backup and recovery is in scope as well.

---

[35] The technology layers are: application, database, operating system, and network.

The following is an example of the logic we would use to take an IT general control supporting the networking layer process out of scope:

> At the networking layer, we evaluate the risk associated with unauthorized or untested changes affecting the financial statements. During the analysis, we conclude that failed networking changes will result in outages, but not undetected financial statement errors. We conclude that networking level changes affecting the financials is low, and we take this process out of scope.[36]
>
> In other words, for financial reporting, networking failures may cause availability issues for SAP. However, this will rarely cause undetected financial statement miscalculations. For this compliance requirement, focusing on the operating system is not relevant.

At this point, we now understand what is in scope and out of scope for the IT general control processes of change, information security, and operations, as well as what those process areas should be monitoring at the application, database, operating system, and network layers. We should now be able to show the GAIT scoping matrix (below) and clearly explain our reasoning as to why they are or are not in scope.

Layer	Change Management	Operations	Security
Application	Yes	Yes	Yes
Database	No	Yes	No
Operating system	No	No	No
Network	Yes	No	Yes

Step 3: Find And Fix IT Control Issues

Now that we understand the critical in-scope business processes and IT services and we know which CIs deliver critical IT functionality, we will drill down to identify gaps in the key IT general control processes that we rely on.

Task 1: Prepare key IT general control processes

For each business process in scope, we go to each layer of the application stack and each in-scope IT general control process (using the GAIT Matrix) and do the following:

- We examine the risks to critical IT functionality, and we determine what IT general control processes are actually in place.

- We work with management to determine whether the existing controls sufficiently mitigate the risk that critical IT functionality could fail, resulting in an undetected error.

For the IT general control processes of change, access, and operations, we need to substantiate that controls exist and are effective. This will enable us to select the control

---

[36] The authors have found from GAIT experience that what will often bring OS change management back into scope is that reliance is placed on OS patches being deployed on schedule. To ensure that this control is effective, we need change management to substantiate that the right patches are deployed on schedule.

objectives necessary to safeguard critical IT functionality and identify gaps in the existing IT systems that require remediation:

- When change is in scope: We must be able to substantiate that no unauthorized changes have been made. Typically, we can substantiate this claim using preventive, detective, and corrective controls to show that all changes were authorized.

- When access is in scope: We must be able to substantiate that no unauthorized access has occurred. Typically, we can substantiate this claim using preventive, detective, and corrective controls to show that all accounts map to authorized users.

- When operations is in scope: We must be able to substantiate that availability and data integrity meet requirements. Typically, we do this by reviewing incidents and interviewing customers, as well as by verifying that disaster recovery tests were successfully executed.

We have identified the key IT general control processes in scope. We have applied them to the IT technology layers in scope. We have identified any gaps, and we have identified specific control objectives that are needed (e.g., objectives selected from COBIT or ISO 27002:2005), and then will initiate corrective actions, described in the next task.

Again, we must be careful to not go off the deep end by doing a bottom-up analysis—saying "here are all the things that can go wrong with technology that create risk." (We will reread the SOX-404 Cautionary Tale again if we forget this.)

Keep in mind that each control activity comes with resource requirements, including full-time equivalents (FTEs) and costs. An "information security purist" may pursue the elimination of all risks. On the other hand, our goal is to treat IT operations and information security resources as precious and scarce, so we will use them where they are the most needed to safeguard organizational goals and objectives.

In other words, we are prioritizing the risks to the business and tackling them in order of priority.

Task 2: Initiate corrective action

Now, we prioritize and initiate corrective action for the control weaknesses found in the previous step. We want to sort our list of corrective actions by critical nature of the risk, or the magnitude of the residual risk.[37] We are aware that fixing some of these issues will take time. Phase 1 was spent just trying to get oriented and plugged into the organization. Up to now, Phase 2 has primarily been spent on trying to understand what is important. We started building mastery over change and access controls in Phase 1, but we will not start building quality into the IT applications until Phase 3.

Broadly speaking, corrective action for each CI falls into three categories:

- **Stay the course**—Management has full understanding of the level of risk and acknowledges acceptance, so we take it off our list after formally documenting the decision.

---

[37] Many numerical methods exist for prioritizing corrective actions, and are not presented here. Business management and auditors can us help prioritize what needs to be fixed first.

- **Replace/repair the asset**—The decision is made to replace or repair the asset outright, which we can increasingly influence as we integrate with development in Phase 3. Here are two examples:

  A firewall is no longer under maintenance. The vendor has been out of business for six years. The risk is that we cannot make changes without fear of catastrophic failures, and known vulnerabilities exist that may allow unauthorized access through known exploits. We make the decision to purchase and implement a new firewall within three months and migrate the firewall rules over.

  An application that was developed in house was prematurely deployed into production and has developers logging in on a daily basis, due to urgent business changes and break/fix work. Because of uncontrolled changes, the application is prone to failure and the IT operations team does not want to support it. We decide that there is an unacceptable risk of human error and fraud due to the absence of controls around development and change management. We make the decision to create a stable and secure build for the application so it can be operated and maintained by the production team, with no developer access or back doors.

- **Augment controls**—When an IT general process control is deficient, we may make the decision to augment or upgrade compensating controls to better manage the corresponding risk. Here are some examples:

  Audit reviews change management documentation and determines that not all changes are being recorded. An automated detective control is added to identify unauthorized change. It is coupled with a daily reconciliation of the detected change report. Together, these controls correct the deficiency.

  An Oracle database has three programs logging in with privileged access. We either correct the deficiency by reducing the privilege for these program logins, or we compensate for the deficiency by monitoring access and changes made for these login sessions.

  During an actual disaster, it becomes clear that IT cannot recover the main operational systems from tape in the required time because the actual restoration time to full operation required two months. Moreover, some data was not fully recovered because there were not enough tapes. To prevent this from happening again in the future, we implement a corrective plan: we will do regular restoration testing and fix the backup and restore process until we can do complete restores, and we will retest every quarter and after major changes.

Step 4: Streamline IT Controls For Regulatory Compliance

Regulatory and legal compliance are risks that need to be managed. As information security, we need to help bridge the worlds of audit and IT operations by understanding and managing the key control requirements for regulatory and legal compliance. This will enable us to achieve compliance with less audit preparation time and less rework.

During this step, we transition from reviewing controls at audit time (e.g., once per year) to ensuring that we integrate common control objectives required by regulations into the daily operations of relevant IT services. We create a high-water mark of the key IT general control processes required. Then we create a defined schedule when we review and update the needed IT general control process requirements for the high-water mark as regulations change.

By formalizing the process (i.e., documenting inputs, outputs, activities, roles, and responsibilities), we get out of the mode of doing information security work only as time permits (which translates into "rarely, if ever"). We also eliminate the problem of not knowing who does what, or worse, having people work on things that don't matter.

This is sometimes called shifting from "compliance via project" to "compliance via process." Instead of brute-force projects to prepare for upcoming audits, audit and compliance requirements become ingrained into daily operations.

Task 1: Establishing the high-water mark

Next, we identify the high-water mark for the key IT general control processes, establishing minimum targets to ensure compliance across regulations. To do this, we work with corporate counsel and compliance groups to identify applicable regulations and legal requirements. From there, we will then document the required IT general control objectives, and use this information to populate our high-water mark control objective matrix.

The following table illustrates a potential control objective matrix, using COBIT control objectives:[38]

	HIPAA	Sarbanes-Oxley	PCI
AI6.1 Change standards and procedures	(Regulation-specific requirements)	(Regulation-specific requirements)	10.5.1 11
AI6.2 Impact assessment, prioritization and authorization	(Regulation-specific requirements)	(Regulation-specific requirements)	(Regulation-specific requirements)
AI6.3 Emergency changes	(Regulation-specific requirements)	(Regulation-specific requirements)	(Regulation-specific requirements)
DS5.4 User account management	(Regulation-specific requirements)	(Regulation-specific requirements)	(Regulation-specific requirements)
DS5.9 Malicious software prevention, detection and correction	(Regulation-specific requirements)	(Regulation-specific requirements)	(Regulation-specific requirements)
DS5.10 Network security	(Regulation-specific requirements)	(Regulation-specific requirements)	(Regulation-specific requirements)
DS5.11 Exchange of sensitive data	(Regulation requirements)	(Regulation requirements)	(Regulation requirements)

At each column/row intersection, we specify the control objective requirements of the regulation listed in the indicated regulation (column) and the corresponding detailed control objective (row). For each detailed control objective (row), we look for the most

---

[38] Control Objectives for IT and related Technologies (COBIT) is a control framework maintained by the Information Systems Audit and Control Association. http://www.isaca.org/cobit

stringent requirement, which we'll call the high-water mark and use that as the control activity for each key IT general control process we will rely on.

Task 2: Document the IT controls and their monitoring

In this task, we document the IT general control processes to make them repeatable and auditable. We can then use this documentation to communicate the processes required to comply with regulations and train people accordingly.

We will also have to address how evidence of compliance will be generated and stored. We need this evidence to prove to ourselves, management and auditors that we have completed these tasks as specified in the documented processes and that we can substantiate our effort.

We did most of this work of ensuring that sufficient controls exist in change and access processes in Phase 1. Here, our goal is to do the administrative work to streamline the process of mapping IT general control processes back to regulatory requirements and vice versa (i.e., establish and preserve traceability).

For example, we will be able to have the following interaction with an external auditor:

> "So, you're here to do a PCI audit. I notice that you're two weeks ahead of schedule. But that's okay. Here are the business processes that we have identified as in scope, and here is the list of critical IT functionality. Also, here are the IT general control processes that they rely upon, and here is the evidence we have that substantiates compliance with each of your 73 relevant standards."

When we are designing our processes, the following types of documentation needed include:

- The thought process and assumptions made for our scoping decisions.
- Evidence of the identification of key IT general control processes and acceptance by management.
- Policies and procedures with evidence of management's approval.
- Key artifacts from the processes that substantiate the existence of the process and controls, and compliance with the process (e.g., requests for change, information security incident logs, backup schedules, test plans and results, and user acceptance of services into production).

The intent of the documentation is to move beyond rumor, hearsay, and blind trust to management by evidence and substantiated facts. We don't want to drown IT and business groups in a sea of paper. Our goal is to ensure that the right people know what to do, that they do the right things at the right time, and that they are able to substantiate that the right things were done.

We must demonstrate not only that these controls exist, but also that they are effective and adequately monitored. With the production controls that we built in Phase 1, we can easily provide documentation and evidence that substantiates management's assertions that:

- Changes to the system are authorized, tested, documented, and managed into the system.
- Critical data and systems are protected from unauthorized change, etc.

What We Have Built And What We Are Likely To Hear

In this phase, we've leveraged the information we gathered in Phase 1 to establish the scope of information security controls that are needed. The "scope" is in the form of a business worry list of the systems and data that matter most. We've expanded that list to include all externally facing IT infrastructure components. We first implemented reasonable controls to manage the risks associated with externally facing systems so we can begin serious work on the internal controls that address more significant risks.

We examined each business process and system to identify technology risks. We also sought to understand whether there is *reliance* on *critical functionality* on the relevant IT systems. As we progressed, we narrowed our scope to ensure that we spend our time wisely—implementing controls only for systems and data that matter to the business. We ended up with a list of in-scope services to be addressed—that is, services that represent uncompensated information security risks. We prioritized the list according to business impact.

We mapped this list to CIs and drilled down to identify the technology risks so we could identify fragile artifacts and discover assets with unacceptable risks. Then we began taking corrective action to address these risks.

Rather than merely executing the processes defined in this phase as a one-time project, or performed only once a year during audits, we have formalized the processes so that they can be implemented by IT management without drama.

> *"This phase helps information security identify where to focus in a clear and defensible manner, which can then be communicated to and implemented by all the relevant stakeholders."*—STEVE DARBY, VP OF OPERATIONS, IP SERVICES

> *"Recurring compliance and audit issues can be major obstacles to the entire organization, which is what this phase addresses. Using the situational awareness that we gained in the previous phase, we can break the "failing compliance audit" cycle, just as we broke the "failing changes" cycle in Phase 1. By establishing the right priorities, we can focus on creating meaningful policies and controls to meet the business and regulatory objectives. This handbook describes the rough spots and challenges that can significantly reduce audit efforts and outcomes, which management will recognize and appreciate."*
> —PETER PERFETTI, DIRECTOR, IT SECURITY AND RISK MANAGEMENT

Phase 3: Implement Development And Release Controls

What Are We Going To Do?

In Phase 3, we move upstream to the development and release management processes, as well as to the internal audit and project management processes. We will involve stakeholders from development, project management, and release management so they get involved earlier with projects and we will also work with change management, purchasing, and accounting to maintain accurate situational awareness. We will define the model for engaging with individual project groups when there are information security relevant tasks that we can help with.

Issues And Indicators

Visible Ops Security Phase 3 tackles the following issues:

Issue	Narrative Example
Information security and audit do not work together	This afternoon, I had a pretty awful meeting with the internal IT auditor. Several things bothered me. First off, he blindsided me with a whole bunch of deficiencies on password controls for some random systems buried in some business processes that shouldn't even warrant being audited. To make matters worse, he even did a penetration test and hit us with findings from that. And then we ended up getting into a heated debate about IT controls instead of talking about the risks we are trying to mitigate.
	I guess the thing that bothers me most is that we don't appear to be on the same page with respect to what the top business risks are. Consequently, we're having these strange and heated debates about things we should be doing, instead of asking why we should be doing them.
	An objective person watching this argument would have to conclude we are adversaries, each vying for position over the other. Of course, we're actually not, but it sure doesn't seem to me like we have the same goals.
Unless audit and information security work together, progress will be limited	Ideally, I'd like to be able to go in front of senior management and present them with my list of information security risks, and then have audit come in and list the same risks. If our view of the top risks were the same, we could really get some amazing things done by focusing management on what really needs fixing for once!
If audit and information security do not share risk data, they risk failing to protect what really matters	What really bothers me with internal audit is that I know we have huge gaping holes in information security and I want to fix them. Instead, some of these auditors come in and constantly nitpick us on the small stuff, which I then have to resolve because any open audit issues are visible to the board of directors. It's death by a thousand paper cuts.
	Here's what audit hit me with last month: lack of antivirus on a UNIX box that doesn't mount any Windows systems! I don't think that makes any sense at all in our environment, but I'm tempted just to buy something to get them off my back. At least that would close the open audit item that is screwing up our metrics and our year-end performance review.

Issue	Narrative Example
Information security and IT operations pay for the cost of not properly designing services during development	Enough about auditors. Let's talk about how the project management office blew me off on our employee healthcare portal project. All the project manager seems to care about is completing the project on time and within budget. They are under tremendous pressure to get the project completed so it can start generating value. As a result, they seem to do absolutely anything to preserve their date commitment. The resulting level of information security that will actually be in the final release is dubious at best.

This is bad news. The project manager's job ends when the application is deployed. Unlike us, he won't be woken up in the middle of the night after the service goes live. I think I'm going to have to cancel my family vacation next week because we've had three major incidents in the last week. The project team is making decisions that are putting the entire organization at risk.

I wish I could give the project manager a pager so he could fix these problems that the project team members allowed to get deployed. I think that's the only way to get them to understand that if information security controls are weak when the service goes live, both information security and IT operations have to deal with the problems for the rest of their lives. It's no wonder we spend so much time and effort on unplanned work. |
| Attempting to retrofit information security requirements late in projects, or even once in production, is more expensive than addressing them in a planned manner | In my happy, ideal world, I would have been involved in the project right from the beginning, as the system was being designed. Then I could have had a far more rational discussion about the risks early in the life cycle, before even the first line of code was written. And then we could have designed some pretty simple information security controls that would be both effective and sustainable over the long haul.

Instead, we're up at 2:00 in the morning, covering for the sins of the developers. Sure, they are understandably under pressure from tight deadlines. But despite us saving their butts, they still view information security as an important but not required part of their job.

So, we're trying to keep our company off the front page of the newspaper. We've already spent hundreds of thousands of dollars on unplanned and urgent work trying to keep the systems afloat and addressing the information security issues by brute force. We could have avoided so much of this grief if only we could have been involved early in the design and rollout of the releases. |
| Project teams that do not involve information security risk building services contrary to the needs of the organization | For example, let's talk about the last application that the developers put into production. Instead of using the libraries we created to do authentication, they created their own nonstandard libraries, made worse because they haven't been trained on secure programming practices. Now we have to create another piece of complicated middleware to adequately control access.

This unique authentication method now becomes yet another one-off that we need to support. We keep making the mistake of favoring the project goals over the enterprise's goals—over and over again. It has slowly consumed all the air in the room and is killing us. |

Issue	Narrative Example
When management doesn't understand the risks, erroneous decisions can result	When it comes to deployment into production, all I really want to know is what exactly is going into production and when. I want to know that what the development and project teams are delivering is what they promised they would deliver—nothing more and nothing less.
	I'm really tired of functionality being jammed into the release at the last minute. I'm tired of promises of testing only to discover after some digging that they ditched all of the promised QA to preserve the date commitment. Information security was seen as an optional component of the program, and, of course, most of the security "features" were dropped when the deadline came under pressure.
	This application is creating huge risks for the organization. Quite frankly, the people who allowed the application to be deployed made a decision way above their pay grade.
	How do we stop this madness?

In this phase, we will integrate into the processes of four groups: internal audit, project management, software/services development, and release management. We'll be making many phone calls and building relationships to ensure that information security can help them achieve their objectives, as well as those of information security and the entire organization.

Step 1: Integrate With Internal Audit

In Phases 1 and 2, we built an informal relationship with internal audit to enhance our situational awareness. In this step, we integrate more formally into their processes and procedures.

This will be a natural and logical progression of our informal relationship because internal audit and information security already share many similar goals and care about many of the same things. Although auditors must maintain their independence, they also care that IT controls mitigate organizational risk and that IT uses those controls to help achieve operational goals. To prove this to ourselves we merely have to look at the following goals outlined in the Institute of Internal Auditors' code of professional practice[39]:

- Reliability and integrity of financial and operational information.
- Effectiveness and efficiency of operations.
- Safeguarding of assets.
- Compliance with laws, regulations, and contracts.
- Effective organizational performance management and accountability.
- Effective communication of risk and control information to appropriate areas of the organization.

[39] Source: International Standards for the Professional Practice of Internal Auditing, The IIA. http://www.theiia.org/?doc_id=1499

By working with information security, auditors can better maintain their independence and remain outside the management process. By sharing our view of risks and resulting strategy, we can get feedback to ensure that we are looking at the highest areas of organizational risk. As a result, we can reduce the risk of overlooking key areas.

Task 1: Formalize the relationship with audit

Our informal relationship with audit might be characterized as colleagues of general auditors or IT auditors. We meet periodically in the spirit of information sharing so that we can be more effective and efficient in our protection of the organization.

In this task, we formalize the relationship with scheduled meetings between information security and the internal audit team that oversees IT audits. We begin by picking up the phone and calling the person in charge. We introduce ourselves and explain the purpose of our call. Here's how the conversation might go:

"I bet you're tired of having IT management do the bare minimum with respect to controls—following the letter of the law but not the spirit. You're probably also frustrated that IT management fails to protect what matters most, and they do things just to pass audits but fail to implement meaningful controls into daily operations for continual improvement. I can tell you that I'm tired and frustrated by all this too. Would you be interested in discussing how we can work together to address these problems? Or at least come to a common understanding around these issues?"

Our meeting with the head of IT audit includes the following specific agenda items:

- Any audit issues that deal with information security (which should have been routed to us already).
- Any issues that information security has noticed that might be of interest to audit.
- Updates on open issues regarding such items as control weaknesses and remediation efforts.
- Management concerns, such as a late project that has hundreds of contractors staffing it or a merger/acquisition integration effort that has a large IT component.
- Discussion of new or changed IT services going through project and/or change management.
- Reciprocal discussion of top organizational risks (i.e., "So, what's scaring you half to death these days?").

The last bullet tells us where audit believes the largest risks reside. Our goal is not to let audit create information security's agenda. Input from audit, just like input from operations, serves as another source for our situational awareness. Our goal for these meetings is to open and maintain a dialog for sharing of information without fear. This meeting is not a forum for complaining, or the formal review of open or closed issues. It is a meeting of business colleagues to generate a common understanding of business risks.

Task 2: Demonstrate value

When dealing with any group, including audit, we must address the WIIFM (what's in it for me) issue. Here are several ways we can do that:

- Provide domain-relevant expertise around information security. For example, if internal audit needs to audit access controls on Oracle logical security settings, someone on our team may have the necessary expertise. If so, that person can help develop a plan that guides auditors in their review. The goal is not to undermine audit's objectivity. It is to help them understand the technology, associated risks, and the methods for risk mitigation.

- Educate the audit staff, even if we have to fund training. It's a worthwhile investment from an information security standpoint to train key partners with formal (paid) information security training. Training gives people skills that make our job easier. What's more, funding it builds goodwill.

- Share organizational information, information security policies, and standards. We can share documentation that specifies access and configuration standards for applications, operating systems, network devices, and firewalls. An audit team may incorporate this into the audit plan to test both design and operating effectiveness.

- Ensure adherence to daily operational procedures. These standards keep the organization from reverting to the bad old ways. Therefore, we want incorporation of these standards into audit plans so audit can substantiate that they are being followed.

When we do these things well, and have the right relationship with internal audit, we can reduce pressures on audit playing a consulting role. If auditors are the only ones with responsibility for controls, they may be tasked with designing and implementing the very controls that they are responsible for auditing. When they do, they "cross the line," losing their independence and objectivity.[40]

Even when audit serves as the safety net of last resort, audits are not frequent—occurring perhaps only a few times each year. Consequently, control weaknesses may be not be identified until the next audit, leaving the door open to malicious attacks.

Furthermore, we can help management understand the value of controls and integrate them into daily operations. The letter of the law with respect to regulatory compliance has many loopholes that management can exploit to wiggle out of implementing controls that would actually benefit the organization. A director of IT audit once said, "We really missed the boat with SOX. Management used the materiality threshold to exclude many of the IT general control process weaknesses, and slugged it out with both the internal and external auditors to avoid fixing issues that were putting the organization at risk."

---

[40] Norman Marks observes, "In lower maturity organizations, audit has to do more consulting. In higher maturity organizations, audit moves more into an assurance role." But auditors know when consulting is taken too far. The authors are aware of several situations where audit was given budget and a management mandate to "go fix the audit finding." In each case, the auditors were extremely uncomfortable with violating independence and would have preferred that an information security group own remediation. However, audit was the only group with expertise to resolve the problems.

Step 2: Integrate Into Project Management

Many IT organizations have a project management office (PMO) to initiate, prioritize, and manage active and future development projects. Projects are one of the primary means by which organizations achieve goals. New projects help organizations get ahead, and corrective projects help them catch up. Each formal project has a project manager who has primary responsibility (if not sole responsibility) for getting the project completed on time, within budget, and with the specified feature set.

The PMO tracks the health of projects overall, ensuring that the right resources are available and that unauthorized or lower priority projects don't starve critical ones by taking away needed resources. Information security has a vested interest in project management being effective for three reasons. First, most IT controls we implement will be implemented as a project (i.e., they require many steps and often many different people). Second, project management is in and of itself a control. Third, many projects affect the control environment and require reassessing risks and controls based for the new or changed IT service.

In this step, we integrate information security into two primary areas of the PMO function:

- Project initiation and approval processes.
- Key control gates of active projects that have information security implications.

By integrating into the PMO processes, we can start addressing the chronic problem of information security being blamed for late projects and budgets being exceeded. Information security can collaborate with project management by:

- Integrating earlier in projects so we can influence requirements, solution alternatives, design, testing, budgets, staffing, timelines, and expectations.
- Designing information security into applications, which costs far less and is far more effective than attempting to add it retroactively.
- Helping project teams accomplish their objectives and safeguarding the enterprise by providing alternative and potentially creative ways to meet information security requirements.
- Leveraging existing and planned information security services to reduce development, testing, and IT operations workloads.

The PMO can help us secure resources and funding for staff and/or tools to do information security reviews in the early stages of a project. Early participation here is an investment in the future. The payoff for investing more time and resources on proactive efforts is that we avoid wasting time and resources later in reactive efforts when remediation is much more difficult.

The PMO is motivated to work with information security because compliance and security requirements are here to stay. Senior management will increasingly hold project stakeholders accountable for fulfilling these requirements.

Project management and release management teams use templates and checklists extensively to provide consistency across projects and ensure that important requirements are not overlooked. By working with these teams to add sections covering regulatory compliance and information security, we can help them avoid last minute surprises.

What's more, the PMO needs us to ensure that the project succeeds and that critical functionality isn't overlooked or excluded to cut costs and/or time from the schedule. Unaddressed information security risks are often huge. For example, applications lacking encryption, poor user authentication, or applications requiring direct data file manipulation for routine transactions (bypassing application controls such as segregation of duties, program logic, data, referential integrity, etc.).

Applications with inadequate information security can be very costly in time and money after they are deployed. For example, if a production system is not supportable without developer access, it may generate audit issues and require expensive developer rework—which diverts developers from new projects.

Task 1: Participate in PMO approval meetings

The PMO director is typically responsible for managing the portfolio of projects for the organization as well as the project managers. This person is measured on project performance based on factors such as delivering agreed-upon features, meeting due dates, budgets, and all the expectations around them.

It's in our best interest to team up with the PMO director to overcome mutual challenges. So we will pick up the phone and call to introduce ourselves. Here's how the conversation might go:

> *"I bet you're tired of having information security tasks continually making projects late, blowing the budget, and introducing all sorts of unforeseen resource problems. And I bet you're tired of having projects with increasingly complex compliance requirements that are difficult to meet. I sure am. Would you be interested in discussing how we can work together to address these problems?"*

Now that you have the PMO director's attention, ask to be invited to the regular PMO status meetings. Proposed projects are discussed in these meetings before they are officially approved as active projects, which lead to staffing, budgeting, and scheduling decisions. Attending these meetings gives us visibility into the biggest and most important IT projects. For now, we want to understand:

- The project approval process, that is, how project requests become officially authorized projects.
- Which projects seem information security relevant, so we can start thinking about how to get someone from information security embedded in them—or at least in a position to review the project team's work at critical points.
- What projects are currently active, what are the timelines, and who is working on them.

Task 2: Determine information security relevance

We are developing a sense of which projects information security should participate in. But we have to do more to ensure that the PMO recognizes information security as necessary and beneficial, and includes us in projects when appropriate.

Our task now is to define what makes a project relevant to information security. Our goal is to establish basic guidelines, not exact criteria. We want everyone to reach out to information security any time they are working on something that might be relevant. After all, it's better to be paranoid than to learn much too late that a project is indeed security sensitive. Here are potential project criteria:

- Uses authorization or authentication components.
- Uses architecture or technologies that have not yet been evaluated by information security.
- Deals with financial processes.
- Deals with protected health information (PHI) or personally identifiable information (PII).
- Is a high-visibility project that warrants information security's involvement for political reasons.
- Addresses new regulatory requirements or new business risks.
- Changes the way that the business achieves critical objectives (i.e., changes key business process controls or replaces legacy IT services or systems).
- Shares data with third parties.

When projects meet even one of these criteria, the project manager should work with information security to determine if an information security resource should be assigned to the project.

Task 3: Integrate into project review and approval

Project management typically uses a template for project requests—a standardized format that spells out return on investment, the business case, and other relevant factors. Management uses this information to make decisions authorizing and prioritizing projects. It's at authorization time that project managers are assigned, budgets are allocated, and stakeholders are identified. We want to embed information security and regulatory compliance requirements in the request template so management gives them proper consideration for all new projects.

We aren't trying to obtain veto power. We simply want to improve the quality of decisions by ensuring that information security risks and costs are factored in at the early decision-making stages. To do this, we expand our participation beyond status meetings to also include active project meetings. These are the meetings in which the PMO and the responsible project team review project-specific status and issues. The agenda ranges from routine matters (e.g., "everything is fine") to emerging concerns (e.g., discovery of a risk that requires rescoping), to full-blown crises (e.g., running out of time and budget).

We participate in these meetings just in case schedules and/or budgets come under pressure. If we aren't there to advocate the importance of security features or quality assurance tasks up front, there's a good chance these areas will be shortchanged to meet schedule or budget requirements.

The best place to maintain integrity of the projects is at the control gates between project phases. Typical project phases include requirements definition, development, testing, and release to production. The reason a project phase gate provides an excellent control point is that, typically, all stakeholders, including information security, must agree before projects can progress to the next phase.

A policy should be developed for the times when there are more projects than information security resources. In some cases, we can just prioritize and work the projects in order of importance. In other situations, we can temporarily delegate certain responsibilities to other resources. Another option is to develop checklists and hold the PMO accountable to them. Whatever choice is selected, it must balance moving faster with properly managing risk.

We want to ensure that the needs of information security are covered in each project phase. For example, before the requirements phase ends, we want to verify that information security requirements have been appropriately integrated. Similarly, before testing ends, we validate that proper security testing protocols were followed. We should remember that IT operations is also the victim of unplanned work during projects. As a result, information security should encourage, if not require, IT operations involvement.

Overall, we want to monitor the health of projects to identify red flags that indicate the need for rescoping or that reveal pressure to reduce testing, cut functionality, or eliminate other critical elements. Attending project team meetings helps us head off these types of actions that could result in information security risks after the system is deployed into production.

Some projects are clearly security relevant and we need to pay close attention to them. Others may involve specific tasks that warrant information security attention. We need to provide the PMO and project managers with criteria to identify those other projects. Here are several criteria to use:

- The project includes tasks that change authentication, authorization, firewalls, or other important information security controls.
- The project creates risks that could impact organization (e.g., confidentiality, integrity, or availability of information).

We need the PMO or project managers to engage information security when a project meets any of these criteria. We will encourage them to always remember: when in doubt, please consult us because it's better to be safe than sorry.

Task 4: Leverage detective controls in change management

The change management detective controls described in Phase 1 help us maintain our situational awareness, and can tell us when the PMO has been circumvented. For example, change management can detect unexpected spikes in workload or in large-scale requests. Examples include a doubling of RFCs for a specific area reviewed by the CAB, or the sudden appearance of an RFC to install a new mainframe.

These anomalies indicate that some action has been performed, or is being performed, that could be flying under the radar of project management (i.e., an unauthorized project). We verify that there is an unauthorized project and escalate accordingly, because these activities can impact not only security, but also the entire organization.

Task 5: Link to detective controls in purchasing and accounting

Now we want to extend our situational awareness to include purchasing and accounting. This additional coverage will enable us to find capital expenditures for IT equipment and services that were not reviewed and approved by the PMO and/or IT, and prevent these purchases from being completed.

To achieve this, we make another phone call, this time to the controller. Here's how the conversation might go:

"Are you tired of people purchasing IT capital equipment and circumventing proper controls? I know I sure am. I know that all these requests should come only from authorized projects with defined budgets, and I think we both suspect that this isn't always the case. I'd like to help make sure people follow your processes, as well. Could we work together on this?"

In the meeting we will discuss how information security and purchasing might collaborate. Here's an example:

Information security and purchasing review reports of purchases over $10,000 by vendor and department, and investigate items that haven't been appropriately authorized. Assume the groups find two purchase orders, one for a $15,000 tradeshow booth and another for $15,000 worth of nonstandard servers and software that have never been undergone information security reviews.

Although the expenditure levels are the same, the associated levels of risks to the organization as a result of the purchases are not. In the case of the servers, information security and purchasing should know why they were ordered and why standard policies and procedures were not followed.

We can help purchasing and accounting by chasing down the following:

- IT technology purchase orders that did not follow the capital appropriation request policy.
- IT services purchase orders that were not reviewed and approved in advance by IT.
- Invoices that do not tie to approved purchase orders.

Step 3: Integrate Into The Development Life Cycle

Information security and development need each other because it is far more effective and efficient to incorporate information security practices into the software/service development life cycle (SDLC) than to retrofit after the fact. Retrofitting may not even be possible. If it is, it can be tremendously expensive and incredibly burdensome to IT operations, information security, and audit. Retrofits often translate into:

- Wasted time, as developers and IT operations perform unplanned break/fix work.
- Significant information security risks, such as when DBAs must constantly edit tables to maintain normal system operation, bypassing all of the internal application controls.

- Wasted information security efforts, such as the need for information security people to perform time-consuming manual audits of log files to prove that unauthorized access has not taken place.

- Wasted audit time, such as when auditors are forced to substantiate account balances to prove that fraud has not occurred due to poor controls. In the worst case, this is like having to open the warehouse and count all the beans manually because you can't trust the accuracy of the bean counting machine.

Moreover, retrofits delay project completion, cause budget overruns, diminish feature sets, and jeopardize information security goals.

From our standpoint, unless information security, compliance, and IT operations requirements are factored in from the start and development employs secure practices, we will remain in reactive mode. We will fight a never-ending and losing battle. Building quality in from the start avoids these consequences.

From the developer standpoint, it is frustrating to design, develop, and test services only to find out—either just before deployment, or worse, after production release—that the services don't meet all the needs of the enterprise. When this happens, development must perform heroics to accommodate information security and compliance requirements that could have been addressed much more easily and less expensively at an earlier date.

Moreover, developers take pride in their craft and their creations. When design deficiencies allow outsiders to exploit their applications (e.g., a hacker uses malformed data inputs to cause buffer overflows), professional developers will often react with personal anger and embarrassment (e.g., "This is awful! If only someone had told me, I could have prevented this successful attack in a million different ways. I'll fix it right now!")

Furthermore, IT services that are not "designed for IT operations" (e.g., require continual developer access or require direct table maintenance and edits) force IT operations to perform heroics and creates information security risk.

Including information security, compliance, and operational requirements with the business requirements simplifies life for everybody and reduces risk. These requirements can then be implemented like any other features—without last-minute stress and drama.

Task 1: Begin a dialog with development

Development may be done in house or outsourced. Most likely, a combination of these methods will be used. Whatever the case in your organization, someone is in charge. That person, who may have the title of vice president of application development, is typically responsible for the development and maintenance of new services needed by the organization.

We need to find this person and call him. Here's how the conversation might go:

> *"I bet you're tired of information security requirements continually popping up at the last minute and causing all sorts of unforeseen resource problems—not to mention all those audit findings and concerns over hackers putting us on the front page of newspapers. Or maybe you're tired of all the information security issues appearing*

on the radar screen on the very last day of QA. I sure am. Would you be interested in discussing how we can work together to address these problems?"

Our goal is to get information security involved at the earliest stages of the development projects. To get the results we want, we must arm developers with the knowledge and tools they need to establish information security practices for requirements definition, development, and testing.

One way we can do this is by promoting information security training:

- We can fund training of key influencers from our information security budget.
- We can assign an information security liaison to the development team.[41]
- We can purchase application scanning tools and then work with development to review the results and define countermeasures.

Activities such as these influence development to take advantage of information security expertise and capabilities.

Task 2: Establish requirements definition and secure coding practices

In this task, we work with development to define a standard approach for identifying information security requirements during the development life cycle, and we figure out ways to enable development to fulfill those requirements quickly and efficiently. To accomplish this we need to do four things:

1. Develop templates and interface with other groups, such as project management, to ensure that information security and regulatory compliance requirements are methodically collected at the start of each project.

2. Build a repository of information security requirements for specific regulations, hardened libraries,[42] and approved coding practices and patterns. These items help developers avoid writing code or using libraries that have known vulnerabilities that will be detected when information security does its testing. Imagine their reaction when you tell them, "Just use these libraries, and we won't have a repeat of that last project when QA found 12,000 security vulnerabilities, and that information was leaked to all the business and development managers."

3. Establish an agreed-upon protocol that specifies when and how to engage information security, including such criteria as defined in Step 2 with the PMO (e.g., code involving authorization, encryption, financial transactions, and compliance requirements).

4. Identify approved internal and external resources, standards, and guidance for configuration hardening, database security settings, key lengths, and so forth.[43]

---

[41] A formal security liaison will not only help bridge development and security, but also will likely help bridge development and audit.

[42] An application or library is "hardened" when it has undergone security testing and has been configured to minimize risk (e.g., operational tuning, removing of unneeded services, or compiled without debugging enabled).

[43] For more information on the four items above, see CERT's "Build Security In" at https://buildsecurityin.us-cert.gov/daisy/bsi/home.html.

If your organization outsources or procures technologies externally, we need to integrate into the vendor selection and other procurement processes. Information security requirements are equally applicable whether the organization buys or builds. Development can be outsourced, but accountability cannot.

Task 3: Establish secure testing practices

QA and information security have many common goals and values. That commonality can lead to a rich conversation. We pick up the phone, call the QA manager, and say:

> *"Are you tired of QA being resented because you find unexpected features and information security issues that need to be fixed? And are you bothered that QA comes in at the end of the project after the developers have taken up all the time in the schedule and there's never enough time left for those issues to be fixed? I know I sure am. Could we work together on this?"*

Both QA and information security want to ensure that defects are found before systems go into production. We both want development to generate quality code without defects that seriously impact customers.

Often, we information security professionals can augment the QA plan to encompass security testing, including information security requirements testing, capacity testing, and performance testing. At a minimum, we want to provide QA with the following value:

- Information security checklists for applications, operating systems, network devices, and other components.
- Automated testing tools to run against code, builds, and releases.

Again, we can subsidize funding for these items from our budget if necessary. This is also another potential area for an information security liaison to be assigned to help define and oversee security testing.

In some situations, the security testing conducted by QA will be sufficient for us to approve a release. In other cases, we will want to conduct independent security testing. In either case, arming QA with the same tools we use reduces findings and allows more time for correction—at lower cost, with less stress, and with higher success rates.

Step 4: Integrate Into Release Management

To better safeguard the production environment, information security requires standardization and documentation, implementation controls such as checklists, and continual control of production variance. These are also some of the key objectives of release management.

We will strive to reduce variation in the production environment as much as possible. This may contradict what some information security theorists recommend that voice concerns about monocultures, advocating the supposedly inherent safety that diversity provides. However, in the real world, it is difficult to achieve sustainable information security through random diversity. If we use a standardization strategy, we can rely on monitoring and reduction of configuration variance. If we rely on a random diversity strategy, we must rely on luck and obscurity.

To test this conjecture, consider the following thought experiment. Suppose we had to inherit one of two undesirable scenarios. In Scenario A, we would inherit 1,000 servers supporting a given business process, configured identically but insecurely. In Scenario B, we have 1,000 servers supporting that same business process, but each server is configured randomly, but 50 percent are configured securely. Which scenario should we choose?

Some information security practitioners will choose Scenario B. They may give many reasons, including that of monocultures. For example, in biological systems, increased homogeneity in crops results in increased risk of catastrophic crop failures[44]. These information security practitioners may conclude from the biology analogy that the risk of disease is similar to the risk of unpatched and insecure infrastructure, making randomness better than consistency.

On the other hand, let's explore Scenario A, which every high-performing IT organization would choose instead. High-performers emphatically point out that when every configuration is identical, then:

- Our mean time to generate security fixes is lower because we have only one fix to generate.

- We have higher confidence in our fix because we have high configuration mastery of our approved configuration.

- Our mean time to test fixes is lower because we can build one testing environment that faithfully matches the configuration of the production environment.

- Our change success rate is significantly higher because our changes are tested in an environment where we have high configuration mastery.

- Our mean time to deploy fixes is likely much lower because we have a uniform production environment, even allowing us to use automated software distribution tools with high confidence.

The systems in Scenario A also have one very interesting attribute from an information security perspective. The fact that all servers are identical shows that the organization can keep systems in a defined state, as opposed to letting them drift apart over time.

Just how much more expensive in terms of time, effort, and cost is Scenario B over Scenario A? In this thought experiment, we may conclude that if the effort scales linearly with the number of configurations, then Scenario A would require 500 times less effort than Scenario B. That is an astonishing difference in effort (whether it is planned or unplanned), and shows how much more desirable Scenario A is when you have one well-understood configuration.

To achieve configuration standardization, we must integrate into the release management process. Production and information security checklists may exist, but manual performance of the tasks they specify can introduce configuration errors, either in the implementation or the verification phase. What's more, releases may be deployed

---

[44] *They may even cite that virtually all bananas are of the Cavendish variety, and are, therefore, all prone to disease from one strain of fungus. When one gets sick, they all get sick.*

without error into the production environment, but undocumented or unauthorized changes implemented after release may cause configurations to drift from the approved builds. These configuration problems can cause subsequent problems in applying patches and changes.

Release management owns the testing environment. So we want release management to ensure that the production environment matches the preproduction test environment. Will a release into production be successful if the preproduction and production environments do not match and eight weeks of testing were performed? The answer is simple: "It's impossible to predict."

According to ITIL, the focus of release management is "the protection of the live (production) environment and its services through the use of formal procedures and checks."[45] Release management needs information security to influence development to produce reliable software that not only meets customer requirements but also information security requirements. Information security can help release management accomplish this by bringing to bear another source of pressure on development to force process change if necessary.

Like QA, release and deployment management is at the end of the development cycle. When development runs late, release management is often under tremendous pressure to cut corners to help make up for delays in upstream tasks. To compensate, what often gets cut is the testing and rollout planning. Information security can help ensure that the risks of shortcutting release management processes are properly understood and that informed decisions are made.

Release management is one of the key quality processes in ITIL. Release management is tasked with ensuring that all service requirements are understood, tested, and deployed in a way that delivers agreed-upon functionality. It involves testing to pre-approved criteria, obtaining software components from the Definitive Software Library (DSL),[46] release planning, and deployment. By integrating with release management, information security can ensure that all released software is properly authorized via the change management process, and that it is based on stable and secure builds that meet the standards of the enterprise.

Task 1: Formalize the relationship with release management

Integrating information security into all aspects of release management and production acceptance delivers two important benefits: Systems are built and deployed correctly and configurations remain in a known and trusted state after deployment.

So how do we get the ball rolling to make this happen? We work with the release manager, the person responsible for all preproduction activities, such as defining release requirements, planning, testing, obtaining approval from change management, and deployment. Typical titles include Release Manager, Director of Release Management, and

---

[45] This is the definition given in ITIL v2. In ITIL v3 the definition has evolved to be: "The goal of Release and Deployment Management is to deploy releases into production and enable effective use of the service in order to deliver value to the customer." This reflects that we must both deliver and safeguard value in the services we deploy.

[46] In ITIL v3, the DSL is now referred to as the Definitive Media Library (DML).

Director of Preproduction and Testing. We need to find out who the release manager is and pick up the phone and call her. Here is how our conversion might go:

> *"I bet you're tired of release management always being bypassed. Way too often, code that is deployed into production doesn't match the preproduction version and information security requirements are introduced too late in the process. As a result, information security issues appear in production. Well, I'm tired of this, too. All these things could be avoided if people would just stick to the release management process, right? Would you be interested in working together to make this happen?"*

This phone call is our opportunity to schedule a meeting covering how information security can contribute value to the release management process.

Task 2: Ensure standards for secure builds

Secure builds are a combination of mandatory and recommended configurations that reduce the likelihood of operational and information security failures that create vulnerabilities. These vulnerabilities can be exploited by intruders. In this task, we document standards for the creation and maintenance of secure builds.

In these efforts, we want to take advantage of internal expertise as well as external sources to develop internal standards that specify how to harden the builds we release into production or check into the definitive software library (DSL). The Center for Internet Security (CIS)[47] and the SANS Institute[48] are two external organizations that publish information security configuration standards. As these internal standards evolve, we will revise existing documents and/or create new ones so that they can be used across the enterprise, and just as important, so that we don't forget our standards over time!

By necessity, different standards exist for different operating systems, databases, and networking devices. We strive to minimize the number of standards and ensure that no uncontrolled variations slip through.

Typical sources of information security configuration problems include:

- Default settings that enable unnecessary features and modules.
- Unneeded services (e.g., httpd, DNS, and SMB).
- Unneeded open network ports.
- Unnecessary user accounts.
- Default passwords.
- Passwords that need to be changed after development (e.g., developers know the ODBC and application passwords for the new order entry system need to be changed prior to entering production).

Our goal is to help release management effectively find and fix information security concerns such as these prior to storing them in the DSL and/or releasing the new or revised services into production.

---

[47] http://www.cisecurity.org
[48] http://www.sans.org

Applying standards and scrutinizing new software default settings should be incorporated into the release building process to ensure that production systems are safeguarded. Once releases are built, they should be reviewed, approved via the change management process, and checked into the DSL so that they can be leveraged by others. Maintaining releases in the DSL reduces the likelihood of errors and eliminates the need to recreate software components every time they are needed.

Release management should not be the only group setting security parameters. We should create a working agreement with release management to help the group define and implement release information security standards.

Dividing the work between information security and release management makes systems more secure and reduces the chance of error by having information security perform the task of checking the work. By dividing the work, we reduce the risk of assumptions, mistakes, or small "cover ups," and make it more obvious when errors are detected in the release implementation instructions that require rework. We want the release instructions to be accurate and not cause guesswork and/or ad hoc changes during implementation. This attention to detail increases the quality of the releases.

Task 3: Integrate with release testing protocols

We engage with release management to ensure that release packages are tested and information security requirements are taken into account. Development often focuses on specific components. Release management, on the other hand, focuses on collections of components and whether the components work together.

Many of the concepts introduced in Step 3 regarding collaboration between information security and QA also apply here. The information security aspects of release testing often include the following:

- Addition of distributed denial of service attacks (DDoS) testing into load and capacity testing—Ideally this risk is addressed in development. However, it's always better to find these vulnerabilities in preproduction than to be surprised once it is in production.

- Use of vulnerability scanning and management testing tools—Even if these tools could potentially crash applications in the testing process, we should use them anyway. It's better to find the vulnerabilities in preproduction instead of in production. Moreover, it's important to use the same tools in the preproduction and the production environment. That way, we can prepare IT operations for potential problems in the production environment when these tools are run.

- Discovery of the "oh no" moments—For example, you find credit card data stored in plain text or software that IT doesn't currently support.

Early in a project, information security can help contribute to the creation of test cases and, later in the project, can examine the results of testing, whatever that testing may be. Information security contributes value here by helping to solve problems and overcome challenges because information security may have solved similar problems for other projects. Instead of just saying *no*, information security can help everyone get to *yes* (i.e., "If we can't do it this way, why not do X, Y, or Z?").

Task 4: Integrate into production acceptance

Next on our task list is to ensure that the production acceptance checklists and contracts require approval from information security before software is released to production. Before a release or change is approved, there must be a review of the checklist and confirmation that all the required work has been completed. (Of course, we are assuming that there is an approved RFC for the release. If there isn't, refer to the section on unauthorized changes in Phase 1.) At a minimum, organizations should review releases in the change advisory board to obtain final approval for deployment.

We have discussed how release management suffers when there are deadlines and budget pressures because the release process is the last step prior to production deployment. Important decisions are often made at the last minute during final release review and approval meetings. Our job is to provide a policy for exceptions to the release checklist and ensure that decisions are made by the right people at the right levels. For example, is it really okay to deploy without user logins? Is it really okay to deploy without PII data being encrypted? In both cases, how will we formally deal with the exceptions? Do these issues need to be resolved within 30 days or is management willing to formally accept the risks until the next release?

There may be intense business pressure to deploy an application upgrade on schedule. However, the right person must sign off and accept the risks. That person should know if deploying the upgrade is likely to cause operational break/fix issues or information security risks. For example, the upgrade may require two DBAs to fix transactions daily, and while they are fixing the transactions, other business transactions may come to a halt. We should offer this person any alternatives we can that reduce those risks to acceptable levels.

The release process should provide a credible escalation exception process that must be followed to override information security requirements. The escalation process ensures that the decision is made at the right level of management. Information security should not just say no, but rather should ensure that the right people know the risks and alternatives associated with a decision to push a system into production despite reservations.

Lastly, for better or for worse, virtualization technologies (e.g., VMWare, Xen, etc.) enable IT organizations to provision and deprovision IT systems faster than ever. This faster rate of deployment may create considerable risk when information security is not sufficiently involved in the process. For instance, insecure virtual machines can be added and removed from production without us even noticing (e.g., via our scheduled weekly network scans). Consequently, our situational awareness can be significantly compromised, and our required reaction time is compressed even further.

Virtual servers must be properly designed, tested, authorized and audited, even more so than for physical servers. Virtualization significantly reduces the required effort to deploy IT infrastructure, and negates many helpful barriers that helped prevent unauthorized deployment, such as data center access, physical server deployment, cabling, purchasing, and so forth. So, we must ensure that we have adequate preventive and detective controls in place to ensure that virtualized servers follow the defined processes in this step, especially deployment testing and approval.

Task 5: Ensure adherence to release implementation instructions

In high-performing IT organizations, the IT operations staff carries out production rollouts according to release implementation instructions. Following these instructions explicitly ensures information security and operational integrity. Uncontrolled and undocumented change during rollout may introduce unintended vulnerabilities or permit intruders to subvert the production environment.

When there is not full compliance (e.g., implementation diverges from the plan), the entire release should be rolled back via the release's approved rollback plan. Doing so reduces errors and forces the appropriate groups to properly test the release, document all variances, and make necessary corrections. Segregation of duty between release management and data center operations makes this possible.

Task 6: Ensure production matches known and trusted states

Release management's responsibility ends at the moment of deployment. (According to ITIL, change management then will conduct a post implementation review. Following the implementation, configuration management takes over the auditing and verification of production configurations.[49])

Release management has a vested interest in managing the variance between production and preproduction systems. Why? Otherwise, they risk developing builds that have errors, and failing to find them during testing (e.g., preproduction is using a different version of a Java virtual machine with different multithreading attributes or information security models).

Doing this often requires a tool to measure configuration drift and variance against known and trusted states. Any variance should be investigated and the cause of the variance pinpointed.

What We Have Built And What We Are Likely To Hear

We now have an intelligence network for situational awareness and the formal integration of information security into key processes and procedures. We're beginning to hear positive feedback about the role of information security. Information security is perceived as adding value instead of creating roadblocks. The organization is starting to get better visibility of what is in production now and what is planned for the future, and information security requirements are being defined and implemented earlier and with better outcomes. When production systems fail or information security incidents occur,

---

[49] ITIL v3 refers to this as Service Asset and Configuration Management now.

we can recover immediately, quickly identify the causal factors of the failure, and take corrective action to prevent future incidents.

Information security is helping the rest of the organization not just with daily operations, but also planning and strategy.

> *"Virtually every information security practitioner can relate to the frustration when applications being released into production do not meet information security policy or regulatory compliance requirements, and having to accept that there's no time to fix the issues before the release date. We see it coming but are powerless to stop it. And then the audit findings force you back into the dreaded "failing audit" downward spiral. This phase describes how to get out of that downward spiral. Creating meaningful involvement and cooperation of audit, PMO, development, and engineering, we can achieve successful information security. And we can help the entire organization by increasing enterprise stability. We are finally building the quality and stability foundations to fully support information security. Without them, we would quickly revert back to square one. Of course, we'll always get some resistance in completing this phase, but the gains are worth it."*
> —PETER PERFETTI, DIRECTOR, IT SECURITY AND RISK MANAGEMENT

Phase 4: Continual Improvement

The underlying theme for the Visible Ops Security methodology is a joint engagement model in which information security integrates into a variety of key operational processes and procedures. However, our work does not end when we have completed Phase 3. Our goal is to continually improve, focusing on what matters most to help the business achieve its goals. To do this, we need to monitor and measure our progress.

In this final phase, we list measures for each of the phases and tasks that can help measure our short- and long-term progress. We cover key process indicators that describe the achievement of information security objectives, as well as the operational measures that identify whether we're generating value to the business (as opposed to being viewed as shrill, hysterical, irrelevant, and a bottleneck to important work).

High-performing organizations select key performance indicators (KPIs) to not only include performance measures, but also focus on process exception measures. For example, when someone deviates from the defined process in the development and production release cycle, we have a process exception that should be investigated.

For each phase and task, we examine metrics that help us assess the short-term progress and long-term health of the various processes and controls.

Information Security Oversight Committee

Before we start examining the measures associated with each of the three Visible Ops Security phases and tasks, we need to establish an information security oversight committee (ISOC). By holding regular (e.g., quarterly) meetings with management, we can establish whether information security is meeting the needs of the business.

High-Level Information Security Integration Measures

First, we will examine the measures that indicate the success of our interactions with various groups. Examples of these metrics include:

- **Customer satisfaction**—By conducting quarterly satisfaction surveys with each functional group we will gauge satisfaction with information security (on a 1-to-5 scale).[50] We want to keep the survey simple to encourage participation, and make it anonymous if warranted. We always solicit suggestions for improvement.

- **Percent of target operational process integration**—After we identify the total number of processes that we need to integrate with, we can track our progress.

---

[50] The frequency of the surveys depends on many factors including cost, culture, and rate of organizational change.

- **Number of challenged integrations**—This is the number of process integrations that have problems with the functional area working with information security to define how the two groups will work together.

- **Percent of codified process integrations**—Our long term goals should also include formalizing the integration of information security with various processes. In the beginning, we may have *ad hoc* integration based on personal relationships. Over time, however, our interactions should be documented and standardized.

There are additional indicators of increasing success that are simple but effective measures of progress:

- **Invitations to meetings**—As we (information security) build successful relationships with various functional groups, we get invited to more meetings. This may not sound like a good thing to someone who already has too many scheduled meetings. However, it is a good indicator that we are becoming a trusted partner.

- **Soliciting of information security input**—As we build a positive reputation, people go out of their way to solicit our input. This is not just political maneuvers such as asking information security to formally sign off on a recommendation but rather the seeking of our input and feedback that is not necessarily put in writing.

- **Reduction in frequency of audits, audit preparation effort, and remediation efforts associated with audit findings**—As we gain the trust of management, the number of internal audits will likely drop.

Brief Discussion On Metrics

Metrics can be absolute numbers or percentages. Percentages are good for comparison but do not show the volume. A 100 percent change success rate stemming from one recorded change differs substantially from 100 percent of 10,000.

Trends over time can be very important to indicate the health of processes. There are many potential measures from which to draw. We should select measures based on what management deems important, our desired outcomes, and the behavior we want to promote.

The remainder of this phase presents a number of short-term progress indicators and longer-term measures that should be used to gauge the performance improvement of each process and procedure integration point. Short-term indicators and long-term measures are indicated for each task of each step in Phase 1 through Phase 3.

Measures For Phase 1

The objective of this phase is to measure IT general control processes implemented in the production environment.

Step 1: Situational Awareness

Situational awareness builds through three primary levels of understanding:

- **Level 1—basic awareness.** We have enough information to make intelligent judgments on risk based on a basic comprehension of what is going on. This doesn't allow us to fully understand all the intricate relationships between systems or processes, but we know at a high level what the environment looks like. For example, we may know how many Exchange servers there are in the organization. A military analogy of this level is that we are able to identify that there is a large battalion-size unit over the next hill.

- **Level 2—moderate awareness.** We begin to more accurately assess business risks and technology vulnerabilities that jeopardize them across systems and services. For example, we know which Exchange servers are linked to which business units, and that some are used by the 24-hour customer support team. Continuing with a military analogy, we know not only that there is a battalion over the next hill, but also more specific information such as which unit it is and who the commanders are.

- **Level 3—detailed awareness.** We have an accurate understanding of business risks. Because we understand the relationships of systems and services, and the impact of an incident on those systems at a detailed level, we can understand the vulnerabilities and the threats to those assets. For example, we may know which Exchange servers have which patches applied. The military analogy is that we know the details of the battalion unit on the other side of the hill, such as its leaders, how it fought in the past, the status of its supplies, and its combat effectiveness.

Step 2: Integration With Change Management

Short-term progress indicators:

- **Percent of changes (that required information security review) effectively reviewed by information security**—What are the number and percentage of all tracked changes that are reviewed by information security on a weekly or monthly basis? Initial goals for this measure should be set with the change management team. The goals are dependent on information security resource availability to review change requests in a timely manner based on their impact to information security controls and the organizational environment.

- **Number of unauthorized changes investigated**—How many unauthorized changes were successfully investigated by information security or change management?

- **Incidents caused by information security-related changes**—What are the number and percentage of all incidents that are caused by changes initiated by or implemented by information security? Information security should focus on driving down the number of information security-related incidents as a way to show IT operations that information security isn't screwing stuff up.

- **Percent of emergency changes**—Emergency changes typically have more risk than changes that follow the normal process. Due to this additional risk, the volume of emergency changes should be monitored. The lower the number the better.

Long-term measures:

- **Percent of systems that match known, trusted, and approved states (i.e., "golden builds")**—How many production systems match their golden-build definition in an audit? The higher the percentage, the better. This number indicates the amount of change that is taking place outside the change approval process. Unauthorized drift indicates unmanaged change, and that's an information security red flag.

- **Average time required to complete information security investigations**—If this is too long, either we need more staff or we need to make our investigation process more efficient.

Step 3: Reduce And Control Access

Short-term progress indicators:

- **Count of excessive administrator rights**—How many and what percent of all systems have more than two (or another number that is accepted by management as a baseline) admin logins. Restricting administrator access is important to meet information security and production availability objectives.

- **Administrator class profiles approved**—What percentage of administrator-class employees had their access profiles approved by management? Management should approve all administrator class employees for each service.

Long-term measures:

- **Percent of services that have developer production access controlled**—How many services do developers have access to? Over time, administrative or write access by developers should be removed for all production services.

- **Number of user account adds/removes/changes**—The number of account activations, changes, and removals should be tracked and trended over time.

- **Number of ghost accounts**—Number of accounts are left active on a system that shouldn't be (e.g., employee was terminated or service is no longer used).

- **Average time between an employee leaving the organization and IT disabling access.**

- **Number of exceptions found during account re-accreditation.** If this number is high, or trending upwards, it should trigger an investigation.

- **Access policy violations**—New user accounts and job transfers that do not have the requisite management approval documentation. Or transfers that have not been concluded following the completed transition of an employee from one role to another.

Step 4: Information Security Incident Response

Short-term progress indicators:

- **Percent of information security incidents detected by automated control—** Higher is better, as it demonstrates that we are monitoring what matters and, hopefully, detecting incidents before it can turn into a loss event.

- **Percent of information security incidents reported from IT (outside of information security)**—Lower is better. Ideally we want incidents to be discovered within IT.

- **Percent of information security incidents reported from outside IT**—This measure should be lower than the previous. Ideally, we want all information security incidents to be detected by IT, as opposed to the business, or worse, customers outside the business.

- **Percent of information security incidents that result in a loss event (e.g., reputation, financial, or findings)**—Lower is better.

Long-term measures:

- **Information security incidents by severity level**—Tracking the severity level of information security incidents provides trending information that can be used to monitor the changing mix of information security incidents.

- **Count of security fixes (changes)**—Information security should track the number of fixes requested to address security deficiencies. By tracking the number of information security-related change requests, we can monitor the amount of security resolution.

- **Mean time to repair for information security remediation**—What is the average time to restore a service into production once an information security incident has been identified and either the service is brought down purposefully by IT or crashed by malicious activity.

Measures For Phase 2

In Phase 2, we gain more comprehensive situational awareness of business prioritized service and systems. The primary objective is to link system- and process-level information security controls to high-priority business requirements. The continual improvement focus for this phase is on short-term progress and long-term health of business-prioritized situational awareness.

Step 1: Establish Our Business Process Worry List

Short-term progress indicators:

- **List of primary business services**—Do we have a good working list of what's important to the business? The completeness and accuracy of this list is the key indicator of short-term progress for this task.

- **List of disaster recovery (DR) ratings (or Business Impact Analysis ratings)**—Do we have ratings for all the systems on our list?

Long-term measures:

- **Full list of prioritized services**—The long-term measure is having a living list of prioritized systems. The work of compiling and maintaining this list is never finished because systems and priorities constantly evolve. We also need some indicator of how the service contributes to the goal (e.g., how financially material the system is).

- **Date the full list was last verified and updated if needed**—This should happen at least annually and after major changes such as mergers and acquisitions, the deployment of a large scale IT service, etc.

Step 2: Work The List, Zoom Out To Rule Out

Short-term progress indicators:

- **Critical business service technology inventory**—What percentage of critical business services have a complete technology inventory? Each business service should have an inventory of IT services on which it relies.

- **List of regulations and legal obligations associated with each service.**

Long-term measures:

- **All business service technology inventory** –What percentage of all business services have a completed technology inventory?

- **Critical service inventory review**—What percentage of critical services technology inventory is reviewed on a regular schedule? The goal should be to have 100 percent of critical services have a technology review on a defined basis.

- **List of any critical IT functionality that is relied upon for internal control objectives.**

- **List of IT general control processes and control objectives at the four levels of the IT application stack associated with each service (when there is reliance on critical IT functionality).**

Step 3: Find And Fix It Control Issues

Short-term progress indicators:

- **Critical services with IT general control process assessment**—What percentage of critical services had a formal IT general control process assessment looking for gaps? The goal should be 100 percent.

- **Control gaps outstanding** –The percentage of key IT general control processes for critical systems that are deficient and require remediation, and that have been communicated to the groups responsible for remediation. In other words, deficiencies have been communicated to responsible owners.

Long-term measures:

- **Ratio of IT general control process deficiencies closed versus reported**—The long-term goal is to have all reported gaps addressed and closed. The ratio of closed to reported provides an ongoing status indication of the amount of open activity. (To keep this ratio meaningful, we should do this for a given period of time, such as year to date or last audit cycle.)
- **Mean time to repair IT general control process deficiencies**—The average time it takes to close each deficiency identified.
- **Percent of repeat audit findings**—Lower is better.

Step 4: Streamline It Controls For Regulatory Compliance

Short-term measures:

- **Number of relevant regulations identified**—This is the total number of applicable regulations that have been designated as in scope.
- **Percent of critical IT services that have high-water marks for regulatory and legal compliance identified.**

Long-term measure:

- **Percent of controls behind schedule**—This is the percent of IT general control processes that have not been reviewed according to the defined schedule.

Measures For Phase 3

Step 1: Integration With Internal Audit

Short-term progress indicators:

- **Informal conversations**—The best indicator of progress is through conversations with audit outside of formal audit meetings. As an information-sharing practice, we should have frequent casual interactions with audit that are outside the scope of investigations or audits.

Long-term measure:

- **Sharing knowledge**—We should be having regular meetings with audit to exchange information with the objective improving the organization and its ability to achieve business goals.

Step 2: Integration With Project Management

Short-term progress indicators:

- **Percent of projects with information security involvement where information security is needed**—Higher is better.
- **Percent of PMO phase gates with information security requirements**—Higher is better.

Long-term measures:

- **Percent of PMO phase gates with formal information security approvals**—Higher is better.

Step 3: Integration With Development

Short-term progress indicators:

- **Development activity with information security involvement**—The percentage and number of development activities with information security review prior to submission to the change advisory board.

- **Information security requirements in SDLC**—The number of information security requirements identified in the software development life cycle.

- **Secure programming practices**—Secure programming practices are identified and communicated to development resources.

Long-term measures:

- **Secure development training**—The number and percentage of target developers who have had information security training.

- **Percent of new or upgraded applications that went through appropriate security testing cases**—Higher is better.

- **Information security functional requirements defined**—The number and percentage of development activities that have information security requirements built into their overall functional requirements.

Step 4: Integration With Release Management

Short-term progress indicators:

- **Approved builds (i.e., golden build) with information security review**—The percentage of approved build configurations that have had information security review and approval.

- **Percent of releases that have undergone security testing according to policy**—Higher is better.

Long-term measures:

- **Percent of approved build changes that have had information security review**—Higher is better.

What We Have Built And What We Are Likely To Hear

In this phase we have developed metrics to help with our command and control of information security. By tracking metrics and regularly reviewing them, we can gain insight into the health of our processes and organization. We can continue to refine information security's ability to safeguard and promote the creation of value.

What we have built:

We are now more integrated with foundational-level activities within the organization, allowing us to target more advanced activities and processes, such as automating some of the processes we have built. For example, through our involvement with SDLC we can create automated components (such as MS Project tasks) to give to project managers that are rebuilt on adaptive self assessments.

What we are likely hear:

Information security is no longer thought of as an outside entity nor does information security have to fight for involvement. We find we are becoming involved in more project and strategic discussions instead of being involved only when problems are discovered. When information security is automatically and without a second thought included in future operations planning, we know we have become part of the team.

> *"Lastly, in Phase 4 the authors outline ways you can measure your success. This is a more important phase than you may realize. You and your management will need to know how you're doing on an ongoing basis. Business goals and objectives change and technology, process, and everything else you do to meet those objectives must change to meet them. Because of all the awareness you've gained along the way and now that you're maintaining it, you can keep stable, flexible and secure infrastructure."*—PETER PERFETTI, DIRECTOR, IT SECURITY AND RISK MANAGEMENT

Summary

Congratulations! By finishing this book, you have learned how to move your organization's information security program towards being a business enabling component of the organization. This book expands on the *Visible Ops Handbook*, which focused on IT operations. Many astute information security professionals immediately recognized that the processes and phases identified in the *Visible Ops Handbook* would directly lead to the protection of the organization's information assets. This understanding led to the creation of this book, which builds upon the concepts of the *Visible Ops Handbook*, additional research and puts an information security perspective on them.

The phases in this book are designed to help the information security function support business goals by focusing on what matters and meaningfully integrating with other functional areas. Whether you are starting a new information security function for your organization, or enhancing an existing one, the phases in this book are relevant to you. It is never too late to begin aligning your information security program to the needs of the business.

It is our sincere hope that *Visible Ops Security* will help your organization in your process improvement journey.

Sincerely,

Gene Kim
Paul Love
George Spafford

The following is an example of the decision matrix wherein we review each layer of the technology stack to understand what the relevant IT general control processes are, the risks they are intended to mitigate, control objectives, and whether the control is in scope for each technology layer (application, database, operating system, and network).

Application layer:

			Answer 3.1
ITGC Area	Risks	Control Objectives	In Scope?
Change	Unauthorized or untested changes are made to the application, interfaces, or reports, resulting in inaccuracies in the data input to the financial statements.	Accruals are completely and accurately calculated.	Yes The likelihood of change impacting the application without change management controls is high.
Operations	Operations is unable to appropriately recover lost or corrupted data due to data backup and recovery failures.	Application data is backed up on a timely basis and recoverable in the event that data is lost or corrupted.	Yes. Due to the criticality of the information, recoverability is also is critical.
Security/Logical Access	Inappropriate or unauthorized access to a critical application could impact financial reporting results.	Proper authorization of the account creation or modification is obtained prior to granting access. Terminations are processed in a timely manner and the account is disabled or removed. Unique passwords are utilized, meeting the minimum requirements of the organization.	Yes. Fraud risk is sufficiently high that we need to rely on restricted access.

Database Layer

			Answer 3.2
ITGC Area	Risks	Control Objectives	In Scope?
Change	Unauthorized or untested changes are made to the database, interfaces, or reports, resulting in inaccuracies in the data input to the financial statements.	Accruals are completely and accurately calculated.	No. Changes to the database are rarely made.
Operations	Operations is unable to appropriately recover lost or corrupted data due to data backup and recovery failures.	Application data is backed up on a timely basis and recoverable in the event that data is lost or corrupted.	Yes. Due to the criticality of the information, recoverability is also critical.
Security/Logical Access	Inappropriate or unauthorized access to a critical database could impact financial reporting results.	Proper authorization of the account creation or modification is obtained prior to granting access. Terminations are processed in a timely manner and the account is disabled or removed. Unique passwords are utilized, meeting the minimum requirements of the organization.	No. The database resides on a server hosted by the third-party vendor and access is restricted to the third-party vendor DBA. Past SAS 70 reports have indicated controls in this area are operating effectively.

Operating System Layer

ITGC Area	Risks	Control Objectives	In Scope?
Change	Unauthorized or untested changes are made to the operating system, resulting in inaccuracies in the data input to the financial statements.	Accruals are completely and accurately calculated.	No. The operating system is hosted by the third-party vendor and there are no changes made to the operating system other than standard patch management procedures. Past SAS 70 reports have indicated that controls over patch management have been operating effectively.
Operations	Operations is unable to appropriately recover lost or corrupted data due to data backup and recovery failures.	Application data is backed up on a timely basis and recoverable in the event that data is lost or corrupted.	No. Not applicable.
Security/Logical Access	Inappropriate or unauthorized access to a critical operating system could impact financial reporting results.	Proper authorization of the account creation or modification is obtained prior to granting access. Terminations are processed in a timely manner and the account is disabled or removed. Unique passwords are utilized, meeting the minimum requirements of the organization.	No. The operating system is hosted by the third party and operating system security would have a remote chance of impacting the application or the database.

Network Layer

			Answer 3.4
ITGC Area	*Risks*	*Control Objectives*	*In Scope?*
Change	Unauthorized or untested changes are made to the operating system of the network switches, resulting in inaccuracies in the data input to the financial statements.	Accruals are completely and accurately calculated.	Yes. Changes to the upload script could result in corrupted or erroneous data transmissions.
Operations	Operations is unable to appropriately recover lost or corrupted data due to data backup and recovery failures.	Application data is backed up on a timely basis and recoverable in the event that data is lost or corrupted.	No. Not applicable, loss of the upload script and data could easily be reconstructed.
Security/Logical Access	Inappropriate or unauthorized access to a critical network switch operating system that could impact financial reporting results.	Proper authorization of the account creation or modification is obtained prior to granting access. Terminations are processed in a timely manner and the account is disabled or removed. Unique Passwords are utilized that meet the minimum requirements of the organization.	Yes. Security needs to be in place to protect the encrypted transmission.

Summarized GAIT Matrix Summary

Layer	*Change Management*	*Operations*	*Security*
Application	Yes	Yes	Yes
Database	No	Yes	No
Operating system	No	No	No
Network	Yes	No	Yes

- **Application controls:** Controls within an application that limit the risk of fraud or human error, causing the application to perform in a manner other than designed. Examples include reasonableness checks, lookup tables, authentication, and so on.

- **Availability:** Typically stated as the ratio of the time that the system or service is operating within acceptable bounds divided by the total possible time.

- **Basel II:** The second of the Basel Accords, which are recommendations on banking laws and regulations issued by the Basel Committee on Banking Supervision.

- **Business:** Includes private sector enterprises as well as nonprofit organizations and government entities.

- **Business goals:** The reasons that the organization exists. Examples include: to maximize return on shareholder equity, to provide quality patient care, and so on.

- **Computer Emergency Response Team (CERT):** CERT is located at Carnegie Mellon University's Software Engineering Institute. This group studies internet vulnerabilities, research long-term changes in networked systems, and develop information and training to help improve security.

- **Change Advisory Board (CAB):** A defined group of stakeholders with vested interests in the system(s) in question. CAB members are able to weigh the risks and benefits of change while maintaining proper communication.

- **Commercial Off-The-Shelf (COTS):** A term for software or hardware, generally technology or computer products, that are ready made and available for sale, lease, or license to the general public.

- **Configuration Item (CI):** One discrete build that is tracked. It may be a base component that can not be further divided or an assembly made up of other configuration items. CIs can be hardware, software, documentation or a combination thereof.

- **Configuration Management Database (CMDB):** A system used to track configuration items, requests for change, work orders, errors, relationships, etc. The definition is often nebulous as the exact implementation varies across organizations. Fundamentally, it is the core system(s) that tracks all activities including service levels.

- **Control Objectives for Information and related Technology (COBIT):** COBIT is an IT governance framework and supporting toolset that allows managers to bridge the gap between control requirements, technical issues, and business risks. It is published by the IT Governance Institute®.

- **Database Administrator (DBA):** A person responsible for the environmental aspects of a database.

- **Definitive Software Library (DSL):** A repository of authorized software that is secure and has version control. Software may only be added or removed from the library through formal processes.

- **Distributed Denial of Service Attack (DDoS):** This occurs when multiple compromised systems flood the bandwidth or resources of a targeted system. Systems are compromised by attackers using a variety of methods.

- **Electronic Data Interchange (EDI):** A particular set of standards for computer-to-computer exchange of information or a set of standards for structuring information that is to be electronically exchanged between and within businesses, organizations, government entities, and other groups.

- **Enterprise Application Integration (EAI):** The uses of software and computer systems architectural principles to integrate a set of enterprise computer applications.

- **Enterprise Resource Planning (ERP):** Organizational planning in the utilization of resources (people, money, assets, etc.).

- **Enterprise Risk Management (ERM):** The methodology and supporting processes that allow for consistent application of risk treatment such as risk avoidance, mitigation, acceptance, and transfer.

- **Federal Information Security Management Act of 2002 (FISMA):** A U.S. federal law enacted in 2002 as Title III of the E-Government Act of 2002. The Act was meant to bolster computer and network security within the federal government and affiliated parties (such as government contractors) by mandating yearly audits.

- **File Transfer Protocol (FTP):** FTP is a commonly used protocol for exchanging files over any netTCP/IP based network to manipulate files on another computer on that network regardless of which operating systems are involved (if the computers permit FTP access). There are many existing FTP client and server programs. FTP servers can be set up anywhere between voice servers, internet hosts, and other physical servers.

- **Full Time Equivalent (FTE):** A full-time employee of an organization. (In the United States, this is traditionally someone who works at least 40 hours a week.)

- **Generally Accepted IT Principles (GAIT / GAIT-R):** GAIT is a set of principles and related methodology that facilitates the cost-effective scoping of IT general control assessments. The IIA developed GAIT to help organizations identify key IT general controls where a failure might indirectly result in a material error in a financial statement. More specifically, GAIT enables management and auditors to identify key IT general controls as part of and as a continuation of the company's top-down, risk-based scoping efforts for Section 404 compliance.

- **Ghost Images:** This is a method of converting the contents of a hard drive, including its configuration settings and applications, into an image, and then storing the image on a server or burning it onto a CD or DVD. Ghost images are useful for duplication of systems for deployment or restoration to a golden build.

- **Golden Build:** The authorized production build. It is sometimes called the approved build.

- **Gramm-Leach-Bliley Act:** Legislation by the U.S. Congress that repealed the Glass-Steagall Act, opening up competition among banks, securities companies, and insurance companies. The Glass-Steagall Act prohibited a bank from offering investment, commercial banking, and insurance services.

- **Health Insurance Portability and Accountability Act (HIPAA):** Title II Administrative Simplification provisions require the establishment of national standards for electronic healthcare transactions and national identifiers for providers, health insurance plans, and employers. The Administrative Simplification provisions also address the security and privacy of health data.

- **Human Resources (HR):** This functional area within the organization deals with hiring, firing, training, and other personnel issues.

- **Hypertext Transfer Protocol Daemon (httpd):** A computer program that is responsible for accepting Hypertext Transfer Protocol (HTTP) requests from clients, which are known as Web browsers, and serving them HTTP responses along with optional data contents, which usually are Web pages such as HTML documents and linked objects.

- **Hypertext Mark-up Language (HTML):** Predominant markup language for web pages.

- **Information Security/Infosec/Security:** Terms used throughout the book to describe the business unit tasked with safeguarding organizational goals in the domain of information.

- **Information Security Oversight Committee (ISOC):** A group of senior managers within an organization (or their designees) charged with oversight of an information security program, including alignment with business objectives, sustainability of the information security program, and other functions involved in the alignment of information security to the organizational objectives.

- **Information Technology Infrastructure Library (ITIL®):** A set of concepts and techniques for managing information technology infrastructure, development, and operations.

  ITIL is published in a series of books, each of which cover an IT management topic. The names *ITIL* and *IT Infrastructure Library* are registered trademarks of the United Kingdom's Office of Government Commerce (OGC). ITIL gives a detailed description of a number of important IT practices with comprehensive checklists, tasks, and procedures that can be tailored to any IT organization.

  ITIL v2 was refreshed and published as ITIL v3 in May of 2007. The major difference between v3 and its predecessor is that v3 has adopted an integrated service life cycle approach to IT service management, as opposed to organizing itself around the concepts of IT service delivery and support.

- **International Organization for Standardization (ISO 27002:**2005): A specification for information security management designed to ensure the selection of adequate and proportionate security controls that protect information assets and give confidence to interested parties.

- **Intrusion Detection System (IDS)/Intrusion Prevention System (IPS):** Intrusion detection systems generally detect unwanted manipulations of computer systems, mainly through the Internet, and malicious behaviors that can compromise security. This includes attacks against vulnerable services, host-based attacks, unauthorized logins, and access to sensitive files.

- **Intrusion Prevention Systems** are security devices that monitor network and/or system activities for malicious or unwanted behavior and can react in real-time to block or prevent those activities.

- **IT General Control Processes (ITGC):** A term defined in the GAIT Principles and Methodology developed by the Institute of Internal Auditors (IIA). GAIT consists of four principles that are consistent with the methodology described in the Public Company Accounting Oversight Board's Auditing Standard No. 5:

  1. The identification of risks and related controls in IT general control processes (e.g., in change management, deployment, access security, and operations) should be a continuation of the top-down and risk-based approach used to identify significant accounts, risks to those accounts, and key controls in the business processes.

  2. The IT general control process risks that need to be identified are those that affect critical IT functionality in financially significant applications and related data.

  3. The IT general control process risks that need to be identified exist in processes and at various IT layers: application program code, databases, operating systems, and networks.

  4. Risks in IT general control processes are mitigated by the achievement of IT control objectives, not individual controls.

- **IT Operations/IT Production/Operations/Production:** Terms used throughout the books to describe the business unit responsible for provisioning, and then continuing the operations and maintenance of IT services.

- **Key Performance Indicators (KPI):** Financial and nonfinancial metrics used to quantify objectives to reflect strategic performance of an organization.

- **Mean Time To Repair (MTTR):** The average time it takes to restore service once an asset has failed or dropped below acceptable service levels.

- **Network Operations Center (NOC):** One or more locations from which control is exercised over a network.

- **Operating System (OS):** At the foundation of all system software, an operating system performs basic tasks such as controlling and allocating memory, prioritizing system requests, controlling input and output devices, facilitating networking, and managing file systems.

- **Payment Card Industry Data Security Standard (PCI DSS):** Developed by the major credit card companies as a guideline to help organizations that process card payments prevent credit card fraud, hacking, and various other security issues. A company processing, storing, or transmitting credit card numbers must comply with PCI DSS or they risk losing the ability to process credit card payments. Merchants and service providers must validate compliance with an audit by a PCI DSS Qualified Security Assessor (QSA) Company.

- **Personally Identifiable Information (PII):** Also known as personal identity information. Any piece or pieces of information that can potentially be used to uniquely identify, contact, or locate a single person or that, when combined or used by itself, represents a threat to someone's confidentiality (as defined by law, contract, or personal expectations of the user).

- **Project Management Office (PMO):** The department or group that defines and maintains the standards of process, generally related to project management, within the organization. The PMO strives to standardize and introduce economies of repetition in the execution of projects.

- **Protected Health Information (PHI):** Under the U.S. Health Insurance Portability and Accountability Act, is any information about health status, provision of health care, or payment for health care that can be linked to an individual. This is interpreted rather broadly and includes any part of a patient's medical record or payment history.

- **Public Company Accounting Oversight Board (PCAOB):** This entity is responsible for oversight of the CPA (certified public accountancy) firms that audit the financial statements of companies publicly listed on the Securities and Exchange Commission (SEC).

- **Quality Assurance (QA):** The activity of providing evidence needed to establish quality in work, and that activities that require good quality are being performed effectively. All those planned or systematic actions necessary to provide enough confidence that a product or service will satisfy the given requirements for quality.

  QA covers all activities from design, development, production, installation, and servicing to documentation. It introduced the expressions *fit for purpose* and *do it right the first time*. It includes the regulation of the quality of raw materials, assemblies, products, and components; services related to production; and management, production, and inspection processes.

- **Request for Change (RFC):** A means of proposing a change to any component of an IT Infrastructure or any aspect of an IT service. It may be a document or record in which the nature and details of and the justification and authorization for the proposed change are entered.

- **Sarbanes-Oxley Act of 2002 (SOX):** A U.S. federal law enacted on July 30, 2002 in response to a number of major corporate and accounting scandals. These scandals, which cost investors billions of dollars when the share prices of the affected companies collapsed, shook public confidence in the nation's securities markets.

  The legislation establishes new or enhanced standards for all U.S. public company boards, management, and public accounting firms. It does not apply to privately held companies. The Act contains 11 titles, or sections, ranging from additional corporate board responsibilities to criminal penalties, and requires the Securities and Exchange Commission to implement rulings on requirements to comply with the new law.

  The Act establishes a new quasi-public agency, the Public Company Accounting Oversight Board, or PCAOB, which is charged with overseeing, regulating, inspecting, and disciplining accounting firms in their roles as auditors of public companies. The act also covers issues such as auditor independence, corporate governance, internal control assessment, and enhanced financial disclosure.

  SOX-404: SOX Section 404 requires management and the external auditor to report on the adequacy of the company's internal control over financial reporting.

Both management and the external auditor are responsible for performing their assessment in the context of a top-down risk assessment, which requires management to base both the scope of its assessment and evidence gathered on risk. IT systems are now critical in financial reporting and thus need appropriate controls to manage risks.

- **Securities and Exchange Commission 10-Q reports (SEC 10-Q):** A variety of reports filed quarterly by companies with publicly traded stocks with the Securities and Exchange Commission.

- **Service Development Life Cycle (SDLC) (Also known as Software Development Life Cycle):** A set of standards that define which services are to be created including requirements definition, programming standards, testing protocols, documentation, and so on.

- **Situational Awareness:** The ability to identify, process, and comprehend the critical elements of information about what is happening to the team with regards to the mission.

- **Systems, Applications, and Products in Data Processing (SAP/ SAP Basis):** SAP is the German company whose comprehensive R/3 product is used to help manage large corporations. SAP Basis is a set of middleware programs and tools that provides the underlying base that enables applications to be seamlessly interoperable and portable across operating systems and database products. In addition to the interface between system elements, Basis components include a development environment for R/3 applications, and a data dictionary, as well as user and system administration and monitoring tools.

- **Virtual Private Network (VPN):** A communications network tunneled through another network and dedicated for a specific network. The distinguishing characteristics of VPNs are not security or performance, but that they overlay other network(s) to provide a certain functionality that is meaningful to a user community.

About the Authors

Gene Kim, CISA

Gene Kim co-founded the IT Process Institute (ITPI) in 2004, and is the CTO and founder of Tripwire, Inc. In 1992, he co-authored Tripwire while at Purdue University with Dr. Gene Spafford. Since 1999, he has been studying high-performing IT operations and security organizations, an organization dedicated to research, benchmarking and developing prescriptive guidance for IT operations, security management, and auditors. This same year Gene co-authored the "Visible Ops Handbook: Implementing ITIL in Four Practical And Auditable Steps". He was a principal investigator on the IT Controls Performance Study project, completed in 2006.

Gene currently serves on the Advanced Technology Committee for the Institute of Internal Auditors (IIA) where he is part of the GAIT task force, which has created guidance on how to scope IT general controls for SOX-404. In 2007, *ComputerWorld* added Gene to the "40 Innovative IT People Under The Age Of 40" list, and was given the Outstanding Alumnus Award by the Department of Computer Sciences at Purdue University for achievement and leadership in the profession.

Paul Love, CISSP, CISA, CISM, Security+

Paul has been in the IT and Information Security field for over 15 years. Paul holds a Masters of Science degree in Network Security and a Bachelor's in Information Systems. He has co-authored three books, contributed to multiple other Linux/Unix books, and has been the technical editor for over 10 best selling Linux and Unix books. Paul is currently the Director of Information Security at a large financial services firm.

George Spafford, CISA, IPRC

George is a Principal Consultant with Pepperweed and an experienced practitioner in business and IT operations. He is a prolific author and speaker, and has consulted and conducted training on regulatory compliance, IT Governance, and process improvement in the U.S., Australia, New Zealand and China. Publications include co-authorship of "The Visible Ops Handbook." George Spafford's *Daily News* is read by more than 2,500 subscribers, including high-level executives from Fortune 500 and leading international companies. George holds an MBA from Notre Dame, a BA in Materials and Logistics Management from Michigan State University and an honorary degree from Konan Daigaku in Japan. He is a Certified Information Systems Auditor (CISA) and holds ITIL Practitioner Release and Service Manager certifications. George is a current member of the ISACA, the IIA, and the IT Process Institute.

CHANGES HAPPEN.

BREACHES HAPPEN.

AUDITS HAPPEN.

TAKE CONTROL WITH THE **ALL-IN-ONE** SOLUTION

FOR **SECURITY** AND

COMPLIANCE

Introducing the Tripwire® VIA™ Suite

VISIBILITY into events across your entire infrastructure

INTELLIGENCE transforms data noise into actionable information

AUTOMATION frees your staff for strategic projects

tripwire
ENTERPRISE

tripwire
LOG CENTER